Improving
Your School
One Week at a Time:

Building the Foundation
for Professional
Teaching and Learning

Jeffrey Zoul, EdD

EYE ON EDUCATION
6 DEPOT WAY WEST, SUITE 106
LARCHMONT, NY 10538
(914) 833–0551
(914) 833–0761 fax
www.eyeoneducation.com

Library of Congress Cataloging-in-Publication Data

Zoul, Jeff.
Improving your school one week at a time : building the foundation for professional teaching and learning / by Jeff Zoul.
     p. cm.
ISBN 1-59667-027-4
1. School management and organization. 2. Teacher-principal relationships. 3. Communication in education. I. Title.
LB2805.Z68 2006
371.2—dc22

                                                    2006009674

10 9 8 7 6 5 4 3

Editorial and production services provided by
Richard H. Adin Freelance Editorial Services
52 Oakwood Blvd., Poughkeepsie, NY 12603-4112
(845-471-3566)

Also Available from EYE ON EDUCATION

Great Quotes for Great Educators
Todd Whitaker and Dale Lumpa

Elevating Student Voice:
How To Enhance Participation, Citizenship, and Leadership
Nelson Beaudoin

Stepping Outside Your Comfort Zone:
Lessons for School Leaders
Nelson Beaudoin

What Great Teachers Do *Differently*:
14 Things That Matter Most
Todd Whitaker

Motivating & Inspiring Teachers
The Educational Leader's Guide for Building Staff Morale
Todd Whitaker, Beth Whitaker, and Dale Lumpa

The Principal as Instructional Leader:
A Handbook for Supervisors
Sally J. Zepeda

Instructional Leadership for School Improvement
Sally J. Zepeda

Six Types of Teachers:
Recruiting, Retaining, and Mentoring the Best
Douglas J. Fiore and Todd Whitaker

Data Analysis for Continuous School Improvement
Victoria L. Bernhardt

Handbook on Teacher Evaluation:
Assessing and Improving Performance
James Stronge & Pamela Tucker

Supervision Across the Content Areas
Sally J. Zepeda and R. Stewart Mayers

The ISLLC Standards in Action:
A Principal's Handbook
Carol Engler

Free Downloads

This book displays 37 "Friday Focus" memos each of which provides insight into a specific aspect of teaching and learning for all to reflect on throughout the year. If you have purchased this book, Eye On Education grants permission for you to download each of the 37 Friday Focus memos from our web site. They can be opened in Microsoft Word©. Further permission has been granted to those who have purchased this book to modify and customize the Friday Focus memos so they can fit the specific needs and context of your school. You can access the free downloads by going to Eye On Education's web site:

www.eyeoneducation.com.

Search for **Improving Your School One Week at a Time: Building the Foundation for Professional Teaching and Learning,** by Jeffrey Zoul and follow the directions regarding "Free Downloads."

Book buyer access code: **IMPRZOUL027-4**

Dedication

This book is dedicated to my daughter, Jordyn Campbell Zoul. No one knows more than you how much I love teachers. Yet, of all those great teachers with whom I have worked, you, my friend, have taught me the most. May you work hard, laugh often, and learn always. Use your own strong foundation to build that ladder to the stars.

Foreword

I am honored to write the foreword to this book because the story Dr. Zoul tells about the Otwell school community in Georgia reaffirms my own beliefs about what constitutes great teaching and its inevitable companion, high levels of student learning. Several years ago, I had the pleasure of speaking with Jeff after addressing to a gathering of school principals. Jeff shared with me then much of the good work he was already engaged in at his own school as we discussed school culture, climate and effective communication. We discussed my own ideas and experiences regarding the Friday Focus memo format for communicating with teachers and I encouraged Jeff to use this as a basis for sharing the passion he so evidently embodies about this noble profession called education. At that time, I had no idea that this conversation would find as its ultimate conclusion the book that you are about to read.

The words of wisdom contained in *Improving Your School One Week at a Time* relate to nearly all aspects of K-12 education. This book clearly shows how a large school faculty came together as one to focus on raising academic achievement while simultaneously establishing and building collegial relationships. I have consistently maintained that it is our people, not our programs, that make our schools great. This book provides confirmation that my long-held belief remains sound and it provides a map for others to follow as they set out to build, as Dr. Zoul suggests, a "foundation for professional teaching and learning." All of the key elements of successful school practices—collaboration, differentiation, assessment, professional learning communities, essential components of effective teaching, and communicating core values and beliefs—are examined within the pages of this worthy volume. While I find myself nodding my head in agreement with much of what Dr. Zoul and his staff have to offer within these pages, I find myself even more inspired by the style with which this advice is shared. What comes through loud and clear when reading this book is a story of a school community passionately dedicated to improving their craft and sharing with each other their best practices, their values, and their classroom triumphs.

I invite school administrators, teachers, and other educational leaders to read this book and apply its wisdom in their own schools. Many schools I visit are working hard to become great schools. Schools that succeed in achieving greatness vary in many ways, but they have two things in common: great teachers and great leaders. Jeff is clearly a great leader. Perhaps his most worthy attribute is the respect he has for great teaching and great teachers. He obviously instills confidence within the teachers at his school and these teachers, in turn, do the same for their students—as well as each other. Whether you read this book from beginning to end or browse around from section to section, I am confident you will learn much about how we can improve our schools. More importantly, you will learn much about how we can improve each other. Courageous leadership is crucial to school reform and passionate teaching is equally vital. Both are evident in this powerful book and I encourage you to both read the contents deeply and follow the example set forth by Jeff as he inspires us to teach and lead with passion.

Todd Whitaker
Indiana State University

About the Author

Dr. Jeff Zoul is a principal with the Forsyth County School System in Cumming, Georgia. Prior to becoming principal at Otwell Middle School, Dr. Zoul served as a classroom teacher for 20 years at the elementary, middle, and high school levels. In addition, he has served as an administrator at all three levels and has extensive coaching experience. He also teaches as an adjunct professor at North Georgia College and State University.

Dr. Zoul has also been published in the area of teacher collaboration and speaks on school climate and culture, building professional learning communities, and positive classroom discipline. He earned his doctoral degree from the University of Alabama and holds additional degrees from the University of Massachusetts at Amherst, Troy State University, and the University of Southern Mississippi.

Dr. Zoul is married to Jill Zoul. They reside in Cumming, Georgia, and are the proud parents of one daughter, Jordyn. Dr. Zoul can be contacted by phone: (770) 887-8134; e-mail jzoul@eyeoneducation.com; or mail: Forsyth County Schools, 605 Tribble Gap Road, Cumming, Georgia 30040.

Acknowledgments

My interest in writing this book is the direct result of having been profoundly and positively impacted by numerous teachers and leaders who are giants in their field and in my eyes. First and foremost, I extend my gratitude to the teachers at Otwell Middle School in Cumming, Georgia. Your passion for teaching and learning inspires and motivates not only your students, but also your principal. While I remain indebted to every teacher at this school, from our head custodian, to our cafeteria manager, to our superstar classroom teachers, four have earned my eternal appreciation for the encouragement and feedback they provided as I wrote this book. Special thanks, then, to Suzanne Korngold, Van Lewsader, Beth Richardson, and Leah Finch. As wonderful as you all are as teachers, you are even more amazing as friends.

I have had the good fortune to be mentored by distinguished educational leaders and scholars. Dr. Ellen Cohan has been a constant source of wisdom, compassion, and the not-infrequent bon mot since the day we first met. Dr. Rose Mary Newton at The University of Alabama also served as a role model, exemplifying my longstanding belief that scholarly research and practical application of such research are of equal import. Mrs. Jane Fuqua has earned my respect and awe by relentlessly adhering to the "do-right" law of leadership.

This book could not have been written without the support of Dr. Todd Whitaker and Mr. Robert Sickles. These two men envisioned this book inside of me before I recognized it there myself.

Finally, I am grateful for the love and support of many family members who sacrificed much while I worked on this book. Thank you for believing in me and in this work.

Table of Contents

Index of Themes

Although the 37 chapters that make up this book touch on a wide range of educational issues which arise at all K–12 schools in the course of the school year, they can be loosely organized into eight primary categories. These categories are presented below, along with the titles of the chapters related to these broad strands. Readers may wish to use this index in addition to the traditional Table of Contents in searching for information pertaining to a particular theme.

School Climate and Culture

Working with Students

Effective Teaching

Management, Operations, Organization

Professional Development

Motivation

Interpersonal Skills

Communication

Introduction

This book is intended to be used primarily as a tool for school administrators, but also for classroom teachers or anyone who is teaching a class of aspiring school leaders. The book is organized around the school year itself and provides educators with a wide variety of insights into how to improve our schools. The centerpiece of each of the 37 chapters that make up this book is a writing, which we call at our school the "Friday Focus." Other educational scholars—most notably Whitaker, Whitaker, and Lumpa (2000)—have used this same terminology, and strongly advocate that principals communicate with staff in writing on a weekly basis. At some schools, principals have used the idea of a Friday Focus simply as a staff memo to inform teachers and others in the school of upcoming events. At our school, we also send out such a memo, but this goes out each Monday under the title, "Thank God, It's Monday." In it, we list staff birthdays, club activities, athletic contests, and other scheduled events, along with a few inspirational quotes and a faculty trivia question. While this weekly communication is a fun and important way to begin each week, the Friday Focus has an altogether different purpose: this is our weekly communication tool providing insight into a specific aspect of teaching and learning for all of us to reflect on throughout the year.

Each week at our school I write—or ask another leader at our school to write—about an issue related to education that impacts all of us who are in this business we call teaching. Our weekly memo is typically between 500–1,000 words in length and is sent out via e-mail to each staff member at our school. This includes all secretaries, custodians, and cafeteria workers. Because they all interact on a regular basis with students, they are teachers, too, and are referred to as such at our school. The memo also is distributed to various school officials working in our central office. Occasionally, I will include the Friday Focus memo in the parent newsletter that goes home each month to students and parents. During the course of the 2004–2005 school year, we sent out one Friday Focus communication each week, 37 in total, all of which are included in this book. We have continued this practice at our school for a second year and have found that it not only informs our teachers of new strategies and best practices, but also builds a sense of collegiality, collaboration, and school pride among our staff.

The title of this book references school improvement and building a foundation for professional teaching and learning. I believe these two concepts are directly related. School improvement is an unattainable goal if those working in the school are not learning and growing professionally. As we created these 37 weekly communications, we were building the foundation for what would become our school improvement plan. Teachers at our school became aware of issues affecting us as teachers as well as our students. We reflected on what was written in these weekly communications in our faculty meetings and in faculty study groups. The creation of a regular "Friday Focus" on a specific issue set the stage for our bigger-picture goal of continuously improving our school. The Friday Focus, then, became a vehicle for school improvement.

Did our school improve as a result of these weekly memos? All evidence indicates that our school did indeed improve over the course of a two-year period during which a Friday Focus was sent out each week. Test scores increased, failure rates decreased, faculty surveys indicated an improved teacher perception of our school, both student and teacher attendance improved dramatically, and student discipline data showed a vast improvement in student behavior. While it is difficult to establish a direct cause-and-effect relationship proving that this significant amount of quantitative data was a result of a weekly Friday Focus, I am convinced that the practice played a key role. As more teachers took an active role in creating and discussing our weekly teaching and learning memos, they began to feel responsible for the learning (on the part of both students and teachers) that was occurring.

In a meta-analysis of research studies examining the impact of principal leadership on student achievement, Marzano, Waters, and McNulty (2005) identified 21 responsibilities of the school leader that correlate to some extent with student academic achievement. Nearly all of these 21 responsibilities are issues that are addressed in a Friday Focus within this book or can be addressed by school leaders through the use of similar Friday Focus memos. Specifically, the Friday Focus tool has dramatically impacted the *culture* of our school as we communicate our shared beliefs. In addition, these writings have gone a long way in providing intellectual stimulation by making our teachers aware of current theories and best practices. Most obviously, perhaps, our Friday Focus writings address the principal's responsibility for communication, establishing a consistent and clear method of sharing ideas among all school stakeholders. Shaping the school culture, providing intellectual stimulation, and communicating effectively are three major challenges facing school leaders. The responsibilities of the school principal are daunting, multifarious, and go beyond even the 21 identified by Marzano, Waters, and McNulty. Through the use of our weekly teaching and learning memos, we have found a way to effectively and efficiently follow through on many of these important responsibilities that indirectly—but profoundly—affect student learning.

Although this book is presented in chronological order, beginning with the very first Friday Focus sent out in early August and proceeding through our final one in May, readers may choose to skip around as they read those that are of greatest interest to them at any given point in time. Principals, I would invite you to choose at will anything I have included in this book, modify the content to suit your own school's needs, and send it out to your faculty members. Many of these writings are of a universal theme, applicable to all of us at any level of education. You may want to begin a similar practice at your school by sending out a few of the writings that follow and then calling on leaders within your school to begin writing original pieces to share with their colleagues.

Teachers, I hope you will take the time to consider the advice contained in these pages. All of these strategies, philosophies, and findings have been written by successful educators with years of teaching experience who share practical suggestions that can be adapted for use by teachers in any subject area or grade level. University professors or system-level leaders working with aspiring administrators, I hope you will share these writings with your students as a way to discuss how we can best communicate to our teachers what it is that we feel most strongly about as educational leaders.

This is not a work examining esoteric educational theories or offering scholarly rhetoric. Although all of the ideas presented in this book are based on sound research and years of actual experience, they are simple to understand and relatively easy to implement. This book is designed to be used as a resource for educators in improving their schools. In what is perhaps his best-known book, Roland Barth (1990) suggests that schools should be improved from *within*. That is the driving force behind this book, a simple, step-by-step plan for teachers and principals working together as change agents for school improvement. We need not necessarily look outside our school walls to find what works; instead, the answer—and the responsibility—lies within each of us who works with students.

Part 1

The First Quarter

In our school system, the school calendar is divided into four 9-week grading periods. Other systems in which I have worked organized the school year into six 6-week periods or simply two 18-week semesters. Of these options, I prefer the idea of looking at the school year as a four-quarter event. Not only does it break down the important business we conduct into more manageable chunks of time, it also brings to mind images of an athletic contest, an apt analogy for much of what we do as teachers and administrators.

In sporting events that are arranged into quarters, the first quarter often sets the tone for what will follow. In schools, this is always the case. The beginning of the school year is of monumental importance. According to Wong and Wong (1998), a school's success throughout the year will be determined by what its teachers and administrators do during the first days of school. For both teachers and administrators, the entire first quarter of the school year is a time for establishing the climate of the classroom and of the overall school. During these weeks, teachers and administrators must focus on setting expectations and motivating those with whom they work. Teachers must clearly communicate to students what it is they will be expecting from them throughout the year and motivating them to meet these expectations by establishing positive relationships.

At the same time, administrators must also set expectations for faculty members. This is a time to let teachers know what is expected of them, both as individual classroom teachers and as members of a team working together for the success of the school. This is also a time to capitalize on the excitement of another new school year. As the year begins, we have yet to experience a parent complaint, a discipline incident, or an ill-timed fire drill. Spirits are running high among the teaching staff as they return for another fall; it is the responsibility of school administrators to maintain this sense of optimism and motivate all teachers to work together to make a difference in the lives of those they teach.

The first quarter of this book includes nine chapters centered on a weekly communication we call the "Friday Focus." At the beginning of the year, it is important to me as the principal that I write the vast majority of these memos myself. The first few weeks are used to communicate core philosophies held not only by me, but also by the majority of our returning staff, so that we are all reminded of our shared vision and values as we embark upon an important journey together. In the first three chapters, I manage to convey several key themes that we will refer to throughout the school year. It is not until Chapter 4 that I actually write about a very specific teaching and learning practice that we all must address at some point: homework.

Seven of these first nine Friday Focus writings are ones that I composed and sent to all teachers myself. Of the other two, one was written by one of our school counselors, and the other by one of our assistant principals. I knew that as the year progressed, I would be turning a greater percentage of these over to other respected leaders within our school to write, but early in the year, it is important that the principal communicate his or her own vision of school success to the school community.

1

Opening Day

The first day of school is not only an exciting moment in time for any educator, it is also a day of nearly unparalleled importance. Each new school year opens with a flurry of activity and tasks that immediately crush the preceding lull. The good news for teachers is that students arrive on the first day of school exhibiting their very best behavior. Even those students with the most challenging backgrounds and checkered discipline histories will put forth what, for them, is their very best effort on the first day of school. It is of paramount importance that, as educators, we do whatever we can to capitalize on this once-a-year opportunity. We must remind each other of a seemingly trite, yet powerfully prophetic cliché: you never get a second chance to make a great first impression.

As principal, I work hard to communicate my expectations for teachers on this all-important day. As a staff, we have already spent time together during our preplanning teacher workdays preparing for the arrival of another new group of students. Now, "spring training" is over and "opening day" has finally arrived. My constant message to teachers during this time is very simple and can be summed up in two words: relationships and expectations.

Relationships and Expectations

Principals must insist that teachers establish firm, fair, and simple expectations at the outset of each school year. Teachers must let their students know that these expectations will be enforced consistently for the remainder of the school year. As one who has taught at the elementary, middle, and high school levels, I know this is a vitally important practice for teachers at all grades. As a high school teacher, I kept my own expectations for students very simple and straightforward. I insisted that all students follow the following five edicts, which they would hear frequently during the remainder of the year.

On Time!

I let students know up front my rigidity relating to promptness. Although I assumed that arriving on time needed no definition, I quickly learned that such is not the case in working with adolescents. As a classroom teacher, I came to define "on time" as having every student already seated when the bell rang.

Every Day!

On the first day of school, I made it a habit to inform my students that I would have perfect attendance for the next 179 days. I encouraged them to set the same goal. Inevitably, incredulous students would demand to know how I could make such a bold claim. I would first use my past performance in the area of attendance as evidence in support of this proclamation. Furthermore, I offered an opinion that a positive mental attitude promotes solid physical health. Finally, once I boldly proclaimed this to my students, I felt compelled to follow through on this pledge and, henceforth, made every effort to maintain perfect attendance throughout the school year.

With Stuff!

Another nonnegotiable expectation of mine as a classroom teacher was that all students must arrive to class with all required materials. Once again, it is imperative that we establish precisely what materials we expect students to have for each and every class session on the first day of school.

Heads Up!

Whenever someone was speaking in front of the classroom—whether it was a teacher or another student—I expected all students to sit at attention with heads up—not resting on a desk or in a palm. In addition, I expected all eyes to be focused on the person speaking.

Don't Leave!

As principals, we preach our expectation for "bell-to-bell" teaching and learning. As teachers, we must pass this expectation on to our students. I let students know that my final expectation was that they would not be allowed to leave class except in the case of a legitimate emergency.

A key to ensuring that students meet expectations similar to those outlined above is that as teachers, we model these ourselves. We should not ask students to exhibit exemplary attendance and promptness if we do not expect this of ourselves. We must establish relationships with students such that they *want* to meet our standards of classroom performance. As principals, we must work in a similar fashion with teachers by establishing clear and precise expectations for teacher performance. Having done so, we must then build personal relationships with teachers in a way that motivates them to meet these expectations, no matter how lofty.

The First Friday

It was time for the first-ever edition of the Friday Focus. As a first-year principal at a large middle school, I felt it important to stress my beliefs that human relations skills are ultimately more important to our success as teachers than any pedagogical expertise we might possess. The teaching profession is predicated on relationships. For the first Friday Focus, I sought to communicate simple, time-proven standards for establishing positive relationships with young people. Not surprisingly, these are the same characteristics required to successfully deal with adults. Suggestions such as admitting a mistake, being able to laugh, and realizing that you cannot please everyone are not necessarily esoteric, highly scientific insights. Yet they are as important—if not more so—than anything else we do as teachers.

The teachers at our school had worked hard preparing for the first day of school. My goal in this Friday Focus was simply to thank them for their efforts, share a brief personal story, and remind them of the importance of simple, everyday human relations skills. With this in mind, I sent out via e-mail to all staff the first of what would become 37 messages related to the noblest profession of all—teaching—over the course of an entire school year.

Friday Focus!

August 13

Schools are not buildings, curriculums, and machines. Schools are relationships and interactions among people.
(Johnson & Johnson, 1989)

I hope everyone enjoyed a productive and enjoyable week of preplanning activities. Although Monday will be my 24th "Opening Day," I never lose the nervous edge I felt on my very first day of school when I began my career as a first grade teacher in Gwinnett County. As we begin a new school year Monday, I hope you share my sense of excitement, rejuvenation, and anticipation of what will be a tremendous year of growth for our students and our staff.

As I will suggest on countless occasions during the course of this year, our success as professional educators will depend to some extent on our specific skills and the breadth of our knowledge base. However, I firmly believe that our character and our human relations skills are even more vital to the ultimate success we experience with our students and our entire school community. Nearly every effective educator I have worked with in my career has excelled in the area of interpersonal skills. Although no list of such traits can be thoroughly exhaustive, I do hope that you will peruse those offered below. Let's focus on these human relations skills as we embark upon a noble journey: teaching young people who need and crave our guidance!

- Be willing to admit when you're wrong.
- Be able to laugh (have a good sense of humor) and cry (display empathy and sensitivity).
- Take time to help others.
- Remember how it felt to be a child.
- Be able to resolve conflicts between people.
- Enjoy working with people of all ages.
- Truly care about others.
- Realize that you can't please everyone.
- Be optimistic about people's motives.

Thank you all for your prodigious efforts this week; thank you all for the human relations skills you already possess and practice daily. Let's remember the importance of these as we progress through this year. I can't wait to see you all in action next week! You hold the keys to success for our students; unlock their hearts and their minds.

Have an outstanding week and knock 'em dead (not literally, of course, Coach McNeese)!

Happy Weekend

Jeff

2

What Makes
a Good Teacher?

I was named principal of Otwell Middle School, located outside of Atlanta, Georgia, several months prior to the beginning of the school year. The first thing I did after being named was to meet individually with all 100 certified and classified staff. In these individual meetings, I asked each person three questions: (1) What are we already good at? (2) In what ways do we need to improve? and (3) What can you do to help? Although these one-on-one conferences required countless hours of time over several weeks, they provided me with a tremendous amount of information about the school I would be leading. One message that kept coming through as something positive and which teachers bragged about was what they referred to as "doing things the Otwell way." In a nutshell, this seemed to mean that many folks on staff were prepared to go the extra mile to ensure that each student experienced academic, social, and emotional success.

The quote I selected to introduce the second Friday Focus of the school year seemed to capture the essence of what it is that created this special feeling among many of our teachers, a shared vision that we were a uniquely good school. While we worked hard to nurture this feeling, we also stressed a message of continuous self-improvement and reflection on how we could be even better. In the first Friday Focus, we zeroed in on human relations skills as opposed to teaching skills; in this edition, I sought to share some basic thoughts on what makes a good teacher. Once again, however, the point is communicated that the characteristics of a good teacher are eerily—though not surprisingly—similar to the characteristics of a good human being.

Command of Subject Matter

The second edition of the Friday Focus touched on three key traits of effective teachers: subject matter mastery, caring about each child as an individual, and possessing distinctive character. Although we tended—especially early in the school year—to focus on traits such as empathy, compassion, and character, I also wanted to communicate that mastery of subject matter is absolutely essential to effective teaching. No matter how much we care about students, if we are not intimately familiar with our subject-area content as well as our state curriculum objectives, we will not succeed. In addition to mastering their individual content areas, successful teachers must have a passion for their areas of expertise. I knew that "teaching with passion" would be a recurring theme at our school throughout the year, and I wanted to communicate early on one of my core beliefs that effective teachers possess and exhibit love and passion for both their students *and* their subject matter.

The Second Friday

In addition to using the Friday Focus as a way to highlight and communicate specific teaching strategies and philosophies to our teachers, another feature I tried to incorporate into our Friday Focus communications was recognizing and praising, without embarrassing, teachers who have gone the extra mile for students or who have earned a special honor or accomplishment. In the first Friday Focus, I closed with a lighthearted joke referring to our football coach (and teacher of the year!); the second one closes with a reference to one of our science teachers. Earlier in the week, a college student had visited my office and introduced herself as a former Otwell Middle School student. She went on to tell me that she attributed her success as a biology major at a prestigious university to the knowledge and inspiration she received from this teacher when she was in eighth grade! Now, this is good news worth sharing. Nearly all teachers pursue a career in education in order to make a difference in the lives of young people. In only the second week of school, we had a vivid and inspiring example of one teacher realizing this laudable career goal, and I wanted every other teacher to also realize the power they have to change lives for the better.

Friday Focus!

August 20

What makes a good school has very little to do with how rich or poor the students are or the type of curriculum that's taught. It has very little to do with special programs, expansive playing fields, huge endowments, snappy uniforms, celebrity alumni, or whether the school is wired to the Internet. What makes a good school, whether it's public or private, religious or nonreligious, charter or noncharter, is a feeling. A feeling shared by the entire staff that their particular school is special. The feeling that their school really belongs to them. (Manna, 1999)

The above quote may not directly tie in to the subject matter of to-day's FF, the characteristics of effective teachers. However, I thought of Otwell Middle School teachers when I came across it. The feeling here is nearly palpable. It truly is special, and it fosters a feeling of ownership among staff and students. Thanks to our teachers, we have created and maintained such a feeling.

While cleaning out some files that were in the main office, I came across an article titled "What Makes a Good Teacher?" (Traina, 1999). Please accept my apologies, therefore, if this is something that has been shared previously, but I found that it rang true—at least in my experience. The author sought to identify characteristics that are consistently cited by students and parents as those exhibited by their very best teachers. They are as follows:

Command of subject matter. Effective teachers know their subject matter inside and out. In addition, they convey a love of, and passion for, their subject matter.

Caring deeply about each student and about that student's accomplishment and growth. Effective teachers take time to consider each student as an individual and a unique learner. They take the time and make the effort to get to know about each student, inquiring of their interests, family, and so forth.

Distinctive character. Effective teachers add a special flavor and zeal to their instruction that creates a memorable impression on their students. Whether it is an eccentric sense of humor or a tragedy overcome, such teachers stand out in the minds of their students.

At Otwell Middle School, we are obviously staffed by teachers with distinctive character who care deeply about each and every one of their students. It is equally apparent that OMS teachers possess a superior command of their respective content areas. As a result, your students will remember you long after they leave us. Should you ever doubt this, just ask Mr. Headrick about his experience this week—wow!

Have a great weekend.

Jeff

3

Effort-Based Ability

In the milieu that is public education today, it is the exception rather than the rule that the majority of students enrolled all come from affluent, two-parent families from predominantly one ethnic origin. Instead, school administrators across the nation serve students and families of increasingly diverse racial, family, and economic backgrounds. As differences in demographics increase, students' intellectual capabilities also differ drastically. Many students at our school arrive for sixth grade already several years below grade level in reading and math. Despite our best efforts as a nation, the achievement gap for many student subgroups seems to be growing into a chasm instead of closing.

Principals must avoid falling into the trap of finding excuses or assigning blame for poor academic performance. Like most principals today, I work at a school with a changing population that brings with it concomitant challenges. At times, it is enticing to point to a large percentage of free and reduced lunch students or the growing number of special needs students as a reason for less-than-stellar achievement. One day early in the school year, I found myself bemoaning the challenges confronting our school that were nonexistent at other schools in our system. Fortunately, my assistant principal chastised me and insisted that I never again mention these challenges to our staff. From that point forward, we committed to sending the message that all of our students could achieve and succeed if they—and we—put forth a concerted effort.

Effort-Based Ability

At our school, we shared with teachers our adherence to three messages supporting our belief in what has been called effort-based ability. During the first weeks of school, we would repeat these on the morning announcements to the entire school. At our Saturday morning orientation camp for incoming sixth grade students and parents, I shared these messages with everyone assembled. The messages took on a life of their own among our staff, and soon they were plastered on most classroom doors and on most classroom walls. Simply put, we committed to three core beliefs communicated regularly to students: (1) your work is extremely important; (2) you can do it; and (3) we will not give up on you (Saphier, 2005).

Not only did our teachers regularly communicate these three tenets of effort-based ability to their students, administrators also shared the same message with teachers. Just as teachers must believe in and give confidence to their students, principals must believe in their teachers. Again, their work is of the most profound importance. We had every confidence that they would succeed. Finally, we were committed to not giving up on them, even during those inevitable times when things appeared bleak.

It is important to note that believing in effort-based ability (for both students and teachers) requires more than simple exhortations to work harder. As administrators, we must teach teachers to train their students that effective effort includes attributes of time, focus, resourcefulness, use of feedback, and commitment. The same holds true in working with teachers. With the ever-increasing responsibilities facing teachers today, simply working harder is not the answer. Instead, teachers must work smarter, and it is incumbent upon administrators to assist teachers in finding ways to work more intelligently and more efficiently.

The Third Friday

Not only do I have the good fortune of working with the finest teachers possible, but I also work with over 900 of the world's greatest middle school students. Our students come in all shapes, sizes, and ability levels. Another core belief to which I subscribe and that I wanted to communicate early on to all staff is that each of these youngsters has at least one thing in common: the ability to put forth effort. With continuous and effective effort, we are convinced that ability will actually grow, as evidenced by gains in academic achievement.

In officially communicating these values to teachers for the first time, I again chose to share a personal, self-deprecating story from my own life, which centers on an educator who had a profoundly positive and lasting impact on me. I also began the Friday Focus with a quote that reminded me of so many teachers on staff, a few of whom I named at the outset. I concluded the message with a call to each teacher on staff to set a goal of changing life for the better for at least one student over the course of the school year. Although we are realistic about just how far behind some of our students are, we are simply unwilling to give up on any of them.

Friday Focus!

Educators who believe in effort-based ability believe that all students can do rigorous academic work at high standards, even if they are far behind academically and need a significant amount of time to catch up. Educators who carry this belief into practice are not unrealistic about the obstacles they and their students face. They simply have not given up. And we know for sure that they will get results if they translate this belief into appropriate practice. (Saphier, 2005)

When you read the above quote, did you think of Mike Sloop? Karen Griffey? Suzanne Korngold? Robin Sellen? Carol Swegman? Some other Otwell Middle School teacher? I could go on, but the point is obvious: part of what makes OMS great is the fact that our teachers believe in our students and will go the extra mile to ensure success for all learners. Schools like Otwell communicate on a daily basis that being smart is "something you can get" and not simply something with which you are born. In schools at which the faculty values effort-based ability, teachers constantly remind students of three crucial messages (Saphier, 2005):

1. "This is important."
2. "You can do it."
3. "I will not give up on you."

Have you ever had someone in your life who believed in you and consistently communicated to you that you were an able, valuable person who could and would do great things? In my high school days, that person was Mr. Bruce Campbell, an elementary school principal I met by fortuitous chance at a National Student Council convention in Marlborough, Massachusetts, in 1977. Mr. Campbell believed in me during a time in my life when—upon reflection—this must have been a rather gargantuan leap of faith. Because of his (seemingly unfounded) faith in me, even against all evidence to the contrary, I forced myself to carry on so that I could achieve my goals. Sixteen years after this man entered my life, our newborn daughter was bestowed with the middle name "Campbell" in honor of all he did for me, namely, convincing me that I was able and valuable. As dedicated OMS teachers, you, too, will have this long-term impact on one or more of your students this year.

Believing that all students have innate capacity and that academic ability can be grown is a foremost tenet of professional learning communities. Obviously, we all are born with innate skills and abilities, but it is effective effort, not such innate ability, that is the main determinant of achievement. To demonstrate effective effort, however, students must understand the attributes of *time, focus, resourcefulness, strategies, use of feedback*, and *commitment* (Saphier, 2005). Although not necessarily stated explicitly in the Quality Basic Education or Georgia Performance Standards curricula, these factors are extremely important to student success, and we must directly teach our students how to manage time, how to focus themselves, how and where to go when they are stuck, how to use feedback, and how to reap the rewards associated with hard work and perseverance. These topics must be interwoven into every curriculum standard we expect our students to master.

If we consistently send these messages to students regarding our belief in effort-based ability, our students—even those most at risk or lugubrious—will begin to believe in themselves and become motivated to be thriving members of our school culture based on aspiration and responsibility. Why? Because someone cares about them...someone wants them to succeed...they know what to work on in order to do well...they know what good work looks like and where their current performance is in relation to it...they know how to exert effort...they believe it would be worthwhile to do well...and they believe they are able to do well.

Once again this year, I charge each of us to a noble calling: to become some young person's Bruce Campbell, inspiring that student to levels of attainment even he or she is uncertain is reachable at this stage of life. *This is important work...you can do it...I will not give up on you!* Not giving up on our students is one of the many ways we *teach with passion* at Otwell Middle School!

Happy Weekend!

Jeff

4

The Dreaded
Homework Dilemma

As a first-year principal, I was fortunate to receive many accolades early in the school year from parents regarding our school's performance and that of our teaching staff. Inevitably, however, all principals receive a certain number of parent calls or visits voicing various concerns or complaints. Early in the school year, the few calls of concern I did receive tended to be centered on homework. A few parents—particularly parents of students in the gifted program—called to share their frustration with the amount of time their children were spending each night completing homework assignments. Several suggested that their children were spending up to two hours nightly on schoolwork. Certainly, administrators want to support teachers who assign daily homework and expect it to be completed, yet oftentimes our students' lives outside of school are as busy as our own. We all must strive for balance. The issue of homework, therefore, is something we discussed early in the school year in faculty meetings, Leadership Team meetings, and discussions with individual teachers.

Small Amounts of Meaningful Practice

As a teacher and administrator, I subscribe to the philosophy that we will teach much more than we will ever assess, but that we will never assess anything we have not taught. Along with the practical issues of time and completion, homework carries with it issues related to teaching and assessing. Are we teaching what it is we are asking students to review at home? Are we assessing this student work? At times, we must all work together as educators to ensure that homework is used for practice and to reinforce concepts we have already taught. In addition, we cannot base a significant portion of a student's grade on homework, or the resulting final grade will include an overemphasis on effort rather than learning. Students who fail to understand key concepts but complete homework may receive overall grades that are superior to students who have mastered these same concepts, yet failed to complete homework assignments diligently.

Teachers who assign homework sparingly and for a specific purpose enjoy more success in terms of both homework completion and student learning. Such teachers are also more likely to provide feedback on the homework assignments they do assign and review. As instructional leaders, we must address the issue of homework in our schools and communicate our philosophy and policies to our parents and students.

The Fourth Friday

This edition of the Friday Focus was the first one related to a specific teaching and learning issue that each teacher must address in his or her classroom every year. Individual teachers' views on homework vary widely at every school with which I have been associated. Some teachers insist on assigning a significant amount of daily homework, while others rarely, if ever, assign homework at all. Often, such wide-ranging disparities in this area are the valid reflection of the content area one teaches. Typically, math teachers assign regular homework, while in language arts, homework may be limited to reading and physical education teachers may assign no homework at all.

While it is challenging, if not impossible, to have a schoolwide homework policy, it is essential that we discuss this issue as a staff and that we arrive at a certain level of consistency and agreement as to our values and behaviors in terms of assigning homework. I often refer to my core belief that in many areas of education, as in all other areas of life, less is more. As the instructional leader, it is important to communicate one's own philosophy regarding homework, while at the same time allowing for teacher autonomy within an acceptable framework. The following Friday Focus addresses these and other points related to homework.

Friday Focus!

September 3

Schooling occupies only about 13% of the waking hours of the first 18 years of life, which is less than the amount of time students spend watching television. (Fraser, Walberg, Welch, & Hattie, 1987, p. 234)

I have never been a huge proponent of copious amounts of homework; my mantra has typically been that it should be assigned in small, meaningful amounts. Yet homework certainly has an increasingly appropriate place in education as students move up in grade level. Certainly, homework extends learning opportunities beyond the classroom and is vastly more enriching than any form of television. Used properly, homework refines and extends student knowledge. In assigning homework and establishing homework policies, I defer to Marzano, Pickering, and Pollock (2001) and pass along their suggestions in this area for your perusal.

Those of you who studied Marzano's high-leverage strategies thru our focused choice staff development last year may well recall much of the following. First, parent involvement in homework should be kept to a minimum. Some studies suggest that when parents assist with homework, minimal and even negative effects may result. Also, the purpose of homework must be identified and communicated. The two obvious purposes should be practice and preparation or elaboration. When assigned for practice, the material must have a high degree of familiarity. Practicing a skill that is unfamiliar may only reinforce errors and misconceptions. It is also important that assigned homework be commented on. Studies show that the effects of homework vary greatly depending on the feedback provided by the teacher. Finally, I find myself in cahoots with the authors' three tenets of classroom practice in assigning homework (Marzano et al., 2001):

1. Establish and communicate a homework policy. This should be done at the outset. Explain to students and parents the purposes of homework, the amount you expect students to complete, consequences for not completing homework, and the amount of parent involvement that is appropriate.

2. Design homework assignments that clearly articulate the purpose and the outcome. Clearly identify the purpose of any homework assignment and communicate that purpose to your students.

3. Vary the approaches to providing feedback. Although the goal is to provide meaningful, specific feedback for all assignments, reality suggests that not all homework will receive the same degree of teacher attention. Try to employ different strategies in this area to help you manage the workload and maximize the effectiveness of homework.

I realize that among a staff of 80 or so teachers, we will inevitably have multiple and divergent views on homework. As for myself, I would endorse small, meaningful amounts that have a clearly identified and communicated purpose and that are commented on in some manner by teachers.

Have a great weekend!

Jeff

5

The Impact of a Teacher

The Fifth Friday

Early in the school year, the main focus of our Friday Focus communications is on values we wish to share with all teachers, hopefully in a way that is motivating and affirming to us all. While many future Friday Focus writings will address specific teaching and learning questions that arise at every school—such as the previous week's memo regarding homework practices—for the fifth edition of our weekly communication, I simply wanted to let teachers know that we all make a difference in the lives of our students.

The influence we have on our students can be, of course, positive or negative. I firmly believe that all teachers—even our mediocre ones—enter the field of education for a noble purpose: to make a positive difference in the lives of young people. At times, whether we are at the elementary, middle, or high school level, it may appear as if our students are not responding to our most valiant efforts to enrich their lives. I feel it is important to celebrate our successes in this area and remind each other of the impact we make. That impact may not manifest itself until years down the road, but any veteran educator can cite numerous examples of students who seek them out long after leaving their classroom to let them know of the impression they made.

Although the main focus of the following writing was to inspire teachers to reflect over a three-day weekend on the impact they would be making in the lives of our students during the weeks and months ahead, I also wanted to reiterate our core values about how we can most effectively make that impact. One way we positively affect our students is by providing a safe, orderly, and well-managed learning environment. Again, our students may not always let us know that this is what they want, yet they thrive in such an atmosphere. Discipline is a constant area of concern for educators at every school. I wanted to remind our teachers to set clear expectations and follow through on them firmly, fairly, and consistently as we go about the more important business of making a difference each and every day. The influence of a teacher is boundless, an exciting, intangible reward that we, as educators, receive.

Friday Focus!

September 10

"Nothing you do for children is ever wasted. They seem not to notice us, hovering, averting their eyes, and they seldom offer thanks, but what we do for them is never wasted." Garrison Keillor

After teaching first grade for four years, I decided to accept a position teaching eighth grade language arts. At first, I mistakenly thought that my eighth grade students did not want to please me as much as my first graders did. I was appalled by their apparent insouciance in terms of my regard for them. Certainly, I surmised, my first graders needed me much more than these young adolescents. Folks, as you already know, nothing could have been further from the truth. The more time I spent with my middle grade students, the more obvious it became that these young adults craved my attention, my guidance, and my approval perhaps even more than my first graders.

Our students at OMS feel the same about you. They need you. They rely on you for instruction, compassion, and consistency. Although it may not always be readily apparent, your students like it when you take control. Your students know that good teachers control their classrooms, and they understand and appreciate the boundaries you set. Middle school students thrive in an atmosphere where the teacher stresses self-discipline and communicates with parents regarding progress in this critical area. They respect teachers who discipline students in a firm yet respectful manner that does not sacrifice a student's dignity. Effective teachers establish a set of clear, though limited, expectations with consequences that are consistently and fairly meted out. Teachers who are well organized tend to have the most disciplined classes. The structure of the classroom prevents a lot of off-task behavior, and students know what to expect from day to day.

Being fair and consistent requires courage on the part of teachers, but students will admire those teachers who stand up for what is right and speak out when they observe unfairness. The curriculum you must cover in your various subject areas is vast and even daunting. However, the values you teach your students may be even more important. Students expect you to have beliefs and opinions not only about your subject matter but also about what is right and what is wrong. Sadly, much of what our students learn from textbooks at this age may be forgotten over time. The life lessons you teach them, however, will last a lifetime! Thanks for expertly imparting unto our students what I consider to be an exceptional and comprehensive curriculum. Thank you also for teaching them relevant lessons about life. You are their role model; you may doubt this at times, but even during these moments of doubt, remember this truth. Our kids are watching us and learning from us within the walls of our classrooms and beyond. Therefore, be firm, be fair, be consistent, and use good judgment. Teach your students what you know, but also who you are. Everywhere I go, I find myself extolling the many virtues of the Otwell Middle School teaching force; thank you all for making this such an easy and sincere act in which to engage!

Have a great *long* weekend!

Jeff

6

Effective Listening

As the principal and instructional leader of the school, I feel it necessary and important to compose and communicate the majority of the school year's Friday Focus memorandums. I make it a practice to write the first six editions of each school year, using these opportunities to communicate core values to both new and returning staff. Most of these initial writings pertain to human relations skills as much as teaching skills. For what would be my final Friday Focus before turning this responsibility over to other school leaders in the coming weeks, I wanted to emphasize another key human relations skill: listening.

Active Listening

With each passing school day, it seems increasingly difficult to attend to only one thing at a time. Many of us are guilty of multitasking to a detrimental degree. Like many educators, I often find myself so overwhelmed with work that I resort to talking on the phone while simultaneously composing an email. While meeting with students, parents, or teachers in my office, it is tempting to answer the phone or glance at an incoming e-mail. In the long run, however, I feel that such practices not only send a horrible message but actually take away time rather than save time, since most of us work much more effectively when focusing on one task at a time.

Prior to arriving at Otwell Middle School, the staff had been trained in the popular FISH! philosophy (Lundin, Paul, & Christensen, 2000), a concept I was also familiar with. One of the simple key messages of this slender but insightful text is the concept of "being there" for our customers. In schools, those customers are our students, our parents, and each other. "Being there" refers to what others call active listening. Active listening is a habit one acquires over time. Like most positive habits, it requires discipline and practice. It is a habit that all effective teachers have adopted. Although at times they may frustrate us, our parents, too, expect and deserve teachers who listen intently to their input and concerns. After all, they know their children better than we do, and we can learn from them. Finally, we must listen to each other. As the year progresses, I want our school to grow in the area of collaboration.

It is imperative that we truly listen to each idea or concern shared by a colleague.

When we practice active listening, we make eye contact, send nonverbal signs that we are interested, and avoid interrupting. By listening actively, we not only help another person by showing we care, but we also help ourselves by gaining new insights into another person's perspective or a difficult issue facing our school. Though a seemingly simple concept, active listening is one worth reminding the staff of near the beginning of the school year.

The Sixth Friday

Four of the next six Friday Focus memos would be written by leaders at my school other than myself. For my final Friday Focus before temporarily turning over the reins, I wanted to both communicate another core value and share two books with staff that in some way related to the topic of effective listening: *To Kill a Mockingbird* by Harper Lee and *The Essential 55: Rules for Discovering the Successful Student in Every Child* by Ron Clark. Encouraging teachers to practice active listening skills not only helps us as educators, it also models for students how we want them to behave. In order for students to learn as much as possible, we want them to be active listeners. By practicing these habits ourselves, our students are much more likely to follow suit.

Friday Focus!

September 17

While large meetings and grand symbolic actions play a part, the most significant change in work culture is accomplished in one-to-one personal interactions. (Sagor, 1992, p. 18)

I do enjoy our faculty meetings and our other large group gatherings, but I understand Sagor's emphasis on individualized interactions playing a key role in the success of any work culture, including school buildings and individual classrooms. This is applicable as we work with each other and as we work with our students and parents. One of the primary skills we must possess in order to establish positive interpersonal relations is the seemingly simple skill of listening. It is of paramount importance that we listen: to our students, our parents, and—perhaps most notably—to each other. As important as it is for us to be active listeners, it is equally important that our students do likewise. Highlight the following aspects of effective listening in your own practice and in teaching your students to listen:

- Make eye contact.

- Give your undivided attention.
- Send nonverbal signals that you are interested and that you care. For example, don't shuffle papers or continue writing when someone is with you.
- Be able to restate or paraphrase what is being said when appropriate.
- Don't interrupt. Although students, parents, and even colleagues may interrupt us, guard against sending the message by interrupting—that you do not have time to listen. (McEwan, 2003)

The more we listen, the more we learn. Listening often allows us to quell erumpent conflicts. Moreover, through engaged listening, we have the opportunity to put into practice a central theme of a favorite book of mine, *To Kill a Mockingbird.* In this classic novel by Harper Lee, Atticus often stresses to his daughter, Scout, the importance of seeing things from the other person's perspective. By effectively listening to others, we enable ourselves to really know another person, thereby improving our little world, however slightly. Encourage your students to engage in the above listening techniques.

I'm a bit old-fashioned, but I always encourage my daughter and all young people to respond to adults by saying, "Yes, ma'am" and "No, sir." I was pleased to find this simple piece of advice listed as Ron Clark's number one rule in his book, *The Essential 55: Rules for Discovering the Successful Student in Every Child.* As a teacher and coach, I expected my students and athletes to respond in such a way. As I stressed to them ad nauseam, this simple act of respectful listening really was not going to change my own life a whole lot. Used consistently over time, however, I knew it would have a positive impact upon their lives. Incidentally, I drove over to the Town Center Barnes & Noble to hear Ron Clark speak and to purchase his new book, *The Excellent 11: Qualities Teachers and Parents Use to Motivate, Inspire, and Educate Children.* I will let you know if it is good; please feel free to stop by and borrow it.

At times, we become so overwhelmed that making the time to truly listen gets shortchanged. I know that I am often guilty of this myself. Thanks for listening to our students, our parents, and each other. Thanks also for letting me know if and when I am not doing the same.

Have a great weekend!

Jeff

7

Bullying Prevention

After having written and distributed the first six Friday Focus communications on various topics myself, I now began asking key school leaders to take a turn sharing their own expertise and passions with our staff. For the first "guest" Friday Focus, I called on one of our counselors, who chose to write on the topic of bullying, a problem existing to some extent at every school.

The Far-Reaching Effects of Bullying

Like many schools across our nation, overt bullying does not appear to be much of a problem at our school. Occasionally, we receive a complaint that one of our students is bullying another. However, official incidents of bullying are few and far between and rarely documented as such. Nevertheless, subtle examples of bullying occur more frequently, even though they may—at first glance—not appear to be incidents of bullying at all. Left unnoticed or unchecked, such seemingly minor situations can erupt into full-scale conflicts with far-reaching effects.

In her Friday Focus, our counselor offered a definition of bullying, along with key statistics regarding bullying and tips for teachers for preventing bullying. She stressed the importance of being aware of this issue by pointing out that bullying has long-term effects on both the victims and the perpetrators. She closed by letting teachers know that she and our other counselor would be conducting classroom guidance lessons on bullying prevention at all grade levels.

The Seventh Friday

Heather Roth is the counselor who wrote and shared this edition of the Friday Focus. At the time of this writing, Heather had served as a counselor at our school for only six weeks, yet I wanted our staff to learn from her and perceive her as a school leader. Whitaker (2002) suggests that when we hire new staff, we should ask ourselves how our current staff can be more like the new teacher as opposed to the other way around. I feel that the new people we hire should be so outstanding that we should all want to learn what this individual has to offer us. Heather is one of many examples of new hires who immediately gained the respect of her colleagues through her knowledge, compassion, and dedication to our school. Armed with the information Heather shared below with our staff, our teachers were reminded of a very serious issue and our school became a safer place in which to teach and learn.

Friday Focus!

September 24

"We need to be the change we want to see happen. We are the leaders we have been waiting for." Mohandis K. Gandhi

Over the last few weeks, the counseling office has been dealing with one particular issue at all grade levels. This issue is bullying. While bullying on the surface may not seem like a huge problem, if it is allowed to continue, it can have far-reaching effects on the bully, the victim, and the school community as a whole. Therefore, we need to work together as a school community to create a positive atmosphere so that bullying will not become a method of destruction.

By definition, bullying is "when a person intentionally inflicts injury or discomfort upon another person through physical contact, through words, or in other ways." This behavior is dependent upon there being a power differential and can be the result of a number of different circumstances. Most bullies have average self-esteem but may have poor coping skills. Bullying is not normally done in large groups, but rather involves a small group of two to three students, often with one negative leader. Victims of bullies are usually overly sensitive, insecure, and physically weaker. They have fewer friends and may be clumsy.

The most disturbing thing about bullying behavior is the long-term effects. Students who are bullies by age 8 are three times more likely to be convicted of a crime by age 30. They are less likely to attend college or to acquire a good job. By the age of 23, 35–40% of male bullies had three or more convictions. On the other side, students who are bullied are found to be more depressed and to have lower self-esteem. They are also more likely to commit suicide if they receive no outside help. Victims of bullies are also likely to build up resentment toward others that may result in violent retaliation later. One of the key findings by the Secret Service Report investigating the various school shootings is that many of the attackers in those incidents felt bullied, persecuted, or injured by others prior to the attack. Given these findings, it is crucial that schools develop a plan to combat bullying behavior so that all students can feel safe and secure in their learning environment. Bullying prevention is one of the key elements to reducing the risk of school violence (Olweus, 1993).

Below you will find a few quick tips on how you as teachers and school personnel can be an agent in bullying prevention:

- Provide supervision of students, especially during unstructured time (e.g., in hallways, the cafeteria, restrooms), when much of the bullying occurs.
- Intervene when you have a suspicion that bullying is occurring.
- Be cognizant of students who are often left alone during breaks, lunch, and so on.
- Demonstrate a consistent attitude of nonacceptance of bullying behavior.
- Communicate with all school personnel regarding observed incidents of bullying so that all can be aware of the issue.
- Hold class meetings with your students, if necessary, to discuss bullying issues.
- Recognize positive acts as often as possible (positive discipline referrals).
- When imposing consequences for bullying, separate the act from the individual.
- Encourage all students to become involved in the prevention of bullying. (Olweus, 1993)

The above tips are just some suggestions of ways teachers and other school personnel can assist in implementing a safe and secure environment for students. We all know that students must feel safe before they can learn; these tips can assist in that endeavor.

During the next month, the counseling department will be providing classroom guidance lessons on bullying prevention for all grade levels. We hope that by presenting this information and opening a dialogue with our students, we will be able to create a school community where bullying will no longer exist. We look forward to working with you on this issue.

Have a restful and relaxing weekend.

Heather

8

School Safety

A safe and orderly learning environment is an essential component of any successful school. In fact, many schools publicly claim safety as part of their school's mission. Too often, we tend to take school safety for granted, particularly at schools in which students come from stable backgrounds with supportive parents who expect their children to behave while at school. As we have all seen in recent school tragedies over the past decade or so, school safety is an issue of importance to teachers and administrators at every single school in our country. All school stakeholders must work together proactively to provide for the safest possible learning environment.

Do I Feel Safe at Our School?

Every school should assign a school safety coordinator. At most schools, this should be the principal or a trusted and experienced assistant principal. I was fortunate to move into a school with a veteran assistant principal who had solid experience as a school safety coordinator. Naturally, I asked him to compose 'the Friday Focus below. He began by telling teachers that asking if he feels safe at our school is a daily practice for him, much like our moment of silence or the Pledge of Allegiance. To answer this daily question, one must consider the many aspects that the word "safety" implies.

Synonyms for "safe" include cherished, fostered, impervious, impregnable, invulnerable, safeguarded, secure, sheltered, shielded, uninjured, unmolested, unthreatened, and watched. All of these safety words apply to educators. We are, first and foremost, in the business of keeping our students safe and protected so that they can learn in a stable environment. Although the school safety coordinator is the person most intent on ensuring that this noble priority become a daily reality, all teachers must be reminded of its importance throughout the year, and particularly near the beginning of each new school year.

As much as we value the physical safety and well-being of our students, we also value their emotional and academic safety. Students must feel safe with those of us who work with them. In the classroom, they must feel safe speaking their minds. As Schlechty (2002) suggests, we must provide a safe environment in which each classroom is both physically and psychologically safe. In a safe learning environment, success is expected and mutual respect exists between and among teachers and students. Fear of harm or harassment from fellow peers or inappropriate treatment from teachers should be nonexistent for all students.

The Eighth Friday

Assistant Principal Scott Feldkamp served as our school safety coordinator during this school year. As his primary reference for the Friday Focus, Scott used our own state's department of education, as well as the United States Department of Education, to highlight both the characteristics of a school that is safe and responsive to children and early warning signs of students who may need our help. While we take the issue of school safety seriously at our school, we tend to poke fun at the safety coordinator for his fanatic attention to all things related to school safety. Later in the year, the staff presented Scott with a fancy black cape with the words "Safety Boy" emblazoned in red upon the back. Scott, meanwhile, continued our tradition of humor in the Friday Focus by mentioning—without naming—a teacher who had recently activated the school fire alarm while toasting bread.

Although we are lighthearted in our approach to many school-related issues, we know that safety is absolutely vital to optimal learning. This 'memo was a nice reminder for all teachers.

Friday Focus!

October 1

"To provide a safe and secure school environment conducive to learning with the cooperation of students, parents, teachers, school administrators, and the community."
Georgia Department of Education School Safety Mission Statement

One of the many roles I have at Otwell Middle School is School Safety Coordinator. It is by far one of the most important roles I play. In order to promote a positive learning environment for all who work and learn in our building—students, teachers, custodians, office employees, cafeteria employees, parents, volunteers, and visitors—the need to feel safe is of first and foremost importance. Before I come into work every day, I ask myself, "Do I feel safe at Otwell Middle School?" Looking at Maslow's Hierarchy of Needs, safety is right at the base of the needs pyramid. The only thing more important than feeling safe, according to this pyramid, is meeting one's physiological needs. In other words, if students did not come to school with their basic needs for air, water, food, and sleep satisfied, they wouldn't care about safety. For the majority of students, these physiological needs are being met. Therefore, if students or others who come to work do not feel safe, learning and productive work may not take place.

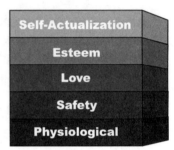

There are many things we as educators can do to help promote a safe learning environment. A school that is safe and responsive to all children will do the following:

- Focus on academic achievement.
- Involve families in meaningful ways.
- Develop links to the community.
- Emphasize positive relationships among students and staff.
- Discuss safety issues openly.
- Treat students with equal respect.
- Create ways for students to share their concerns.
- Help children feel safe expressing their feelings.
- Have in place a system for referring children who are suspected of being abused or neglected.
- Offer extended day programs for children.
- Promote good citizenship and character.
- Identify problems and assess progress toward solutions.
- Support students in making the transition to adult life and workplace. (U.S. Department of Education, 2004)

In addition to promoting these characteristics on a daily basis, listed below are some early warning signs of safety-related issues. The early warning signs are not to be used as a checklist, but rather as a guide in identifying and referring students who may need help. Signs may include the following:

- Social withdrawal.
- Excessive feelings of isolations and being alone.
- Excessive feelings of rejection.
- Being a victim of violence.
- Feelings of being picked on and persecuted.
- Low school interest and poor academic performance.

- Expressions of violence in writings and drawings.
- Uncontrolled anger.
- Patterns of impulsive and chronic hitting, intimidating, and bullying behaviors.
- History of discipline problems.
- Past history of violent and aggressive behavior.
- Intolerance for differences and prejudicial attitudes.
- Drug use and alcohol use.
- Affiliation with gangs.
- Inappropriate access to, possession of, and use of firearms.
- Serious threats of violence.

The answer to the question I ask myself every day is a resounding "YES!" From the custodians walking through and around the building checking for suspicious items each morning to the safety drills we conduct on what seems like a weekly basis, I know that everyone who works at Otwell does everything possible to make it a safer school. I appreciate all the things you do to make school safety a daily reality! (Even those who keep us on our toes while burning yeast, popcorn, or bread in the microwaves!)

Have a great weekend!

Scott

9

Questions, Questions, Questions

With the ninth Friday Focus, we completed the first quarter of the school year. Many of us are surprised each year at how quickly this first significant chunk of the school year whizzes by. As we closed this first quarter, I chose to compose another of my own Friday Focus messages. I also chose to focus on an essential component of classroom instruction: questioning techniques, strategies, and practices.

Effective, Efficient, and Relevant Instruction

A constant refrain of mine is that classroom lessons should be effective, efficient, and relevant. To effect such an outcome, teachers must, unfortunately, plan diligently each day, week, and year. One area that is often overlooked in planning for instruction is questioning techniques. Effective questioning techniques on the part of teachers can dramatically enhance student learning.

Too often, we give little thought to the questioning techniques we use with our students. We either call out questions and accept answers shouted at random, call only on those whose hands are raised, call on the same one or two students in each class, or call on students who are not paying attention as a "gotcha." Used carefully, with forethought, questioning techniques can enhance a lesson's effectiveness, efficiency, and relevancy.

Just as teachers must use questioning techniques expertly, administrators must use questions with teachers to improve instruction or as a means of engaging teachers in self-reflection. In conferencing with teachers about a lesson observation, I sometimes ask three questions: Was the lesson effective? Was the lesson efficient? Was the lesson relevant? For each of these three questions, I also ask, "How do you know?" A lesson is effective if the students master the content. It is efficient if they learn in the least amount of time required to master the skill. It is relevant if the lesson is presented in a way that is meaningful to students.

Although questioning teachers about their lessons can help them reflect on their own practices, the primary focus of this week's memo was to share specific and strategic questioning techniques teachers can and should use in eliciting student responses.

The Ninth Friday

In composing my final Friday Focus of the first quarter, one goal was to set the stage for future Friday Focus writings that would highlight actual classroom teaching practices. In this case, I picked a simple yet important everyday occurrence: teachers using questions to teach students. Too often, we just ask away, with no strategic plan. This writing offered teachers specific ideas on how best to employ various questioning techniques.

As mentioned earlier, we also always strive to invoke a certain amount of humor in the Friday Focus and to personalize the message. I did this by invoking the name of another assistant principal in the questions I made up. Finally, I closed my Friday Focus by including the message that at our school, teachers *Teach with Passion!* By this point in the year, the phrase "Teach with Passion" or "TWP" had become my signature ending to all communications. All subsequent Friday Focus writings I composed closed by tying in the theme of the week to our schoolwide practice and philosophy of Teaching with Passion.

Friday Focus!

October 8

The most basic way teachers have to stimulate interactive thinking and learning in the classroom is through the use of questions.
(Rice & Taylor, 2000)

As a classroom teacher, I often reminded myself that my lessons should be effective, efficient, and relevant. By incorporating focused questioning techniques, teachers can help to ensure effectiveness, efficiency, and relevancy. At OMS, I have enjoyed observing various questioning strategies employed by our adroit teaching staff. Too often, however, questioning becomes an overlooked component of the lesson.

Obviously, through questioning, we check for individual and whole-group understanding (Rice & Taylor, 2000). Questioning individual students is most effective; questioning the whole group is most efficient. At times, it is appropriate to opt for efficiency. When so doing, you might consider using signal responses (teaching students to "show" the answer by a predetermined signal). Questioning individual students is more common and therefore requires greater teacher attention. In questioning, all students should believe that they are as likely to be called on as any other student. In questioning individual students, I find it more effective to utilize an "ask-pause-call" method as opposed to a "call-ask-wait" technique. In the first case, the teacher phrases a question, giving all students time to formulate a potential response. Then, she calls on a random student to provide an answer. Example: "I'm going to ask you a question, and I want everyone to think of an answer. From what you read in our text, what were some causes of the Civil War?"

When calling on an individual for a response, allow ample wait time. Research suggests we should wait 3–5 seconds after asking the question before calling on any individual student (Rice & Taylor, 2000). We should then allow at least 5 seconds for a response and another 3–5 seconds after obtaining a response before reacting. If, after waiting, the student initially does not provide an answer, you might inveigle a response by offering a clue and restating the question. If, after this, the student still had no answer, I would often reply, "That's okay, Suzanne, but pay attention, because I'm coming back to you." Then, I might call on another student to provide the correct answer. Once I received the correct answer, I would return to the original student, getting her to verbalize the correct answer.

On the other hand, by employing a "call-ask-wait" technique (e.g., "Suzanne, what is a noun?"), the resulting effect is that the anxiety level is raised for one student while everyone else is off the hook and not accountable for responding or even attending (Rice & Taylor, 2000). As a teacher, I often found myself reluctant to call on those struggling students who I feared would not be able to respond correctly. By employing an ask-pause-call method of questioning, allowing ample wait time, providing additional clues, and—ultimately—coming back to students who don't initially know the correct answer, I felt that I was able to engage all learners more effectively.

I am pleased, therefore, to note that teachers at OMS are skilled in questioning techniques and avoid capricious patterns of checking for individual and whole-group understanding. Josef Albers stated with perspicacity, "Good teaching is more a giving of right questions than a giving of right answers." Thanks for taking the time to reflect on your daily questioning techniques. *More importantly, thanks for* Teaching with Passion *each day!*

Have a great weekend!

Jeff

Part 2

The Second Quarter

The second quarter of this book mirrors the second quarter of the school year, in that we change our focus from big-picture ideas such as educational philosophies, schoolwide goals, and expectations to more specific topics, including teacher observations and parent-teacher conferences. The second quarter of any school year is also marked by a period of unparalleled activity within the walls of our schools. While there is no point during the year at which we are not furiously engaged in a multitude of teaching and learning activities, the second quarter of the school year seems to encompass an even greater number of "extra" events than other periods throughout the year.

The second quarter of the school year also stands out as unique in that it is during this time that our two most significant holidays occur, Thanksgiving and Christmas. I devote one Friday Focus writing to each of these special times and use these as teaching opportunities with our teachers, much as our teachers do with their students. Both holidays are a time for reflection and renewal as we remember both the good and not-so-good times that have occurred in our personal and professional worlds. Schools are special places in many ways, one of which is the emphasis we still place on holidays and holiday vacations. Administrators can use these special times to remind teachers that we have chosen a noble profession in which to serve. Our influence is profound as we work to make a difference in the lives of young learners.

The following section of this book comprises 10 chapters, each of which includes a Friday Focus written with a specific theme in mind. Of the 10 Friday Focus memos, five are my own; the other five are written by four teacher leaders and one assistant principal. The second quarter of the school year is a time of joyous celebration, yet it can also be a time of stress. For some teachers, the excitement felt at the beginning of the year has evanesced and been replaced with fatigue and the realization that once again, not all of our students are performing to our level of expectation. Some are behaving inappropriately, while others are failing to turn in all assignments. Many of the chapters that follow offer teachers specific strategies for refocusing themselves, their students, and parents on where we stand at this point of the school year and how best to move forward.

10

Parent-Teacher Conferences

No educator can succeed without possessing effective communication skills. Obviously, successful teachers must communicate clearly with the students they teach. Successful teachers are masters at communicating both verbally and nonverbally their expectations for student behavior, their goals and objectives for the courses they teach, what students will learn, and how they will be assessed. As important as it is to communicate clearly to students, it is also vital that teachers communicate regularly and effectively with the parents of the students they teach.

Ironically, some teachers who are completely comfortable standing in front of a classroom filled with all varieties of young learners, holding them in rapt attention are less comfortable meeting with parents. Some are overly shy or uncomfortable pointing out areas in which the student needs improvement. Others react defensively to parent inquiries about what is occurring in the classroom. Still others simply find themselves meeting with an extremely difficult parent or being treated unfairly by an angry parent. Great school leaders take the time to remind teachers about the importance of communicating with parents regularly and how to convene successful parent conferences.

Plan for a Successful Outcome

At the elementary and middle school levels, schools often have scheduled early-release days so that parents can visit with their child's teachers for regular conferences. Unfortunately, at the high school level, regularly scheduled conferences rarely occur. Instead, parents are only invited in to meet with teachers when a serious academic or behavioral problem has arisen. I would encourage teachers at all levels to meet with the parents of each student they teach at least once a year. When this is impossible due to the sheer numbers of students one teaches at the upper levels, it remains important to communicate regularly in other ways with all parents through phone calls;

regular grade reports; postcards sent home in the mail; e-mails; and class, team, or subject-area newsletters.

At our middle school, we have early-release days scheduled for parent-teacher conferences twice a year, once each semester. Since most teachers at the middle school level teach 100 or more students at a time, the amount of time allotted to any single conference must be limited. It is not unusual for parent conferences to be scheduled in 15- or 20-minute blocks, back-to-back, for an entire afternoon and into the evening hours. With such a packed schedule, teachers may become tired and stressed. They may feel as if they are accomplishing little other than superficially highlighting a student's areas of deficiency. To combat all the obstacles that inevitably face us at parent conference time, teachers and administrators must plan for success.

During the first semester, our school system reserves three consecutive early-release days for parent-teacher conferences. These are scheduled for a Wednesday, Thursday, and Friday. At our school, teachers choose to work until 6:00 p.m. both Wednesday and Thursday evenings, conferencing with parents; they make up for this extra duty by leaving early on Friday afternoon. Although this is a stressful and extremely busy week, our teachers look forward to leaving just a bit early on Friday as a small reward for their prodigious efforts throughout conferencing week. This schedule also accommodates parents' busy schedules. By staying late two afternoons, we are able to schedule conferences with parents who are unable to get leave from work.

As principal, I place myself at a desk in the central lobby area of the school and greet parents as they arrive for their conferences. This is a great opportunity for me to meet many of our parents, often for the very first time. I keep a sheet of all scheduled conferences with me and direct parents to their child's classroom. As parents leave their conference, they almost always stop by my table on the way out to share that the conference was a positive experience for them. Many parents also mention that they really like the idea of the principal sitting out front greeting and welcoming all parents.

During the conference itself, teachers work hard to plan for the maximum benefit possible from all this extra effort. Although each teacher or team of teachers has their own way of scheduling and conducting conferences, all of us are expected to follow a few specific guidelines suggested by Partin (2004) in *Classroom Teacher's Survival Guide*. Most importantly, we must decide ahead of time what it is we hope to accomplish. Conference time is not a time for winging it; we should zero in on what problem needs solving and what information we feel we must share with parents to improve the situation. We must choose a limited number of items (no more than three) to tackle at any single conference. I encourage teachers to rehearse what it is they plan on saying. We should greet parents respectfully and cordially as they arrive.

Teachers should stand, shake hands, and address all parents by their last names with titles until they are invited by parents to use their first names. We should treat all parents with dignity and respect and actively listen to their concerns and suggestions. Too often, teachers do all the talking in a conference, when it can be just as productive to allow the parents to do the majority of the talking. One opportunity for listening occurs when teachers inquire about home routines (including bedtime, homework, and responsibilities at home) and about the child's talents and interests outside of school. Finally, we encourage teachers to dress professionally and in a way that reflects the meeting's importance as well as the teacher's respect for the parents and their children.

The 10th Friday

For this edition of the Friday Focus, I asked Van Lewsader, a first-year administrator, to compose and distribute an issue dedicated to the topic of parent-teacher conferences. Although Van was only in his first year as an administrator, he had previously worked as a math teacher at our school and had gained vast experience conferencing with parents. Our conference days were taking place on the following Wednesday, Thursday, and Friday, so this was the ideal time to review a few key components of effective conferences. Throughout his writing, Van stressed the importance of staying positive during all conferences. Finally, he reiterated that effective schools do not limit communication between the home and the school to merely the scheduled conference days; instead, we must practice all forms of clear and consistent communication throughout the school year.

Friday Focus!

October 15

Parent-Teacher Conferences

I'll never forget those anxious, nail-biting moments when my parents—usually my mom—took off for parent-teacher conferences. Even though I was a good student, I still worried. Would I get in trouble for putting pencils in my curly bangs in social studies class to impress the girls? (Yes, I actually had hair at one time.) Would I have to go to the county parks to start my insect collection for science class? The due date was only a few days from now, and in my opinion I had plenty of time remaining to complete the task. Years later, I prepare for my own child's parent-teacher conferences, and I am still nervous. What if my child isn't doing as well as I hoped? What if she's not socializing in class? Will the teacher think I'm a bad parent?

Be positive with people and you'll get positive results (Blanchard, Lacinak, Tompkins, Ballard, & Blanchard, 2002).

As a sports fanatic, I have viewed parent-teacher conferences like a time-out in a game. It is a brief opportunity in a contest (school year) to praise or redirect performances. Todd Whitaker (2004) is known for stating, "Raise the praise and minimize the criticize." A conference is not the time to vividly describe and elaborate on every single minor classroom disruption.

Great teachers help create magical moments and have the ability to ignore minor errors (Whitaker, 2004).

Here are some additional tips for successful conferences provided by the Illinois Education Association (2000). I hope you will keep these in mind as you prepare for next week's conferences:

1. Prepare a conference outline. How are you going to budget your minimal time with parents?
2. Gather student samples for praising and for redirecting.
3. Anticipate possible parent concerns.
4. Provide a comfortable waiting area—chairs, snacks, and reading material such as school or team information.
5. Greet each parent with a handshake and a friendly smile.
6. Explain conference format and goals once seated.
7. Notify parents that you are expected to document all conferences and that a copy will be provided to the parent at the end of the conference.
8. Ask parents if they have any concerns, and reassure parents that their concerns will be addressed.
9. Before addressing any concern, describe students' improvements or successes since midterms.
10. Collaborate when addressing any concern. There should be teacher suggestions as well as parent input. Both parties should agree to this strategy. Suggestions may include more parent involvement by having parents sign daily agendas, graded assignments, or tests. This may mean more teacher involvement also, such as signing agendas, checking notebooks or binders, or having a biweekly phone conference.

11. Review or read documented comments on the conference form to make sure everyone is in agreement.

12. Have parents sign the conference form and keep a copy.

13. End on a positive note.

It is impossible to praise too much as long as it is authentic (Bissell, 1992).

Conferences have provided me with some of my most rewarding moments in teaching. Just as we appreciate praise for our efforts, parents appreciate praise for their efforts and their child's progress. The school calendar may set aside three days for parent-teacher conferences each year. However, I believe great teachers know that parent-teacher conferences are held throughout the entire school year. A great teacher keeps the student, the team, and the parents informed at all times.

Happy Weekend!

Van

11

Student-Led Conferences

The following Friday Focus appeared just as our first scheduled parent-teacher conferences concluded. However, as a follow-up to this regular and important event, I wanted to have teachers give some thought to what our gifted teachers were doing in the area of conferencing with parents—and students. One teacher, in particular, had been a leader within our school system in promoting the idea of student-led conferences as an alternative to the traditional parent-teacher conferences. She had experienced a great deal of success with this concept; after observing the process firsthand during our conference days, I asked this teacher to compose a Friday Focus on the topic.

Holding Students Accountable for Their Own Learning

One of the key benefits to the concept of student-led conferences is the extent to which we get students involved in, and hold them accountable for, their own learning. In today's educational milieu of high-stakes testing and teacher accountability, it is natural to invite students to become more aware of what it is we want them to learn and whether or not they are learning it. Like every other new idea in education, student-led conferencing carries with it both advantages and disadvantages for teachers, students, and parents. For teachers, both an advantage and disadvantage is the amount of effort required on their part. Although student-led conferences can make the teacher's job easier in many ways, this is only the case if the teacher works tirelessly on the front end to plan for efficient and productive outcomes.

The ultimate success of student-led conferences depends on how well the student is prepared for them. At least initially, this level of student preparation is the responsibility of the teacher as much as the student. However, if implemented over time throughout the K–12 spectrum, students become comfortable with the process and more effective at describing their own learning, including their areas of strength and weaknesses. In our school system, this movement began with a small number of teachers across the system, primarily at the elementary and middle school levels. It has gained momentum to the point that a small number of schools have adopted the concept as their primary method of conferencing with parents about their child's progress.

At our own school, we had only a handful of teachers who were implementing student-led conferences, but I had received enough positive feedback from parents, students, teachers, and other administrators to sense that this idea could really improve our school by involving students actively in their own learning. Ironically, successful student-led conferences start with the teacher. The teacher must begin the year preparing students for these conferences. Teachers may decide to host the student-led conferences individually or as a team of teachers across grade levels, core teams, or subject areas. Teachers must help students create a portfolio of learning products collected throughout the grading period. Shortly before the conference dates, teachers should send home a letter to parents informing them that their child will be leading the session. A few days before the conference, each student should meet with the teacher to jointly decide on what evidence from the portfolio should be shared and reviewed with parents. Finally, teachers should have students role-play the conference prior to the event itself. Oftentimes, the teacher will pretend to be the student, modeling how to explain a certain grade, standardized test score, or project to their parent, role-played by the student.

We have discovered that the number one benefit of student-led conferences is the extent to which students become accountable for their own education. Many of us who have taught for years recognize the statement that the best way to truly learn something is by teaching it. By leading their parents in a conference about their academic progress, students are truly learning what their education is all about. Student-led conferences also increase parent attendance at conference time. We have found that parents are much more likely to attend conferences in which their child is the key participant. At the close of each student-led conference, students should share with their parents their goals for the next grading period and their plans for achieving these goals.

The 11th Friday

When asking colleagues to contribute to the Friday Focus writings, I rarely give direction as to what topic to write about. Instead, I merely allow the leaders in our school to share whatever insights are most important to them with the rest of the staff. This week, however, was an exception. Cathy Helmuth taught gifted language arts at our school and was a driving force behind the systemwide student-led conferencing movement. As we were just concluding our first conference days, I asked Cathy if she would share her experiences related to student-led conferences with the rest of us.

I like to think that no staff works harder at traditional parent-teacher conferences than our own. Yet one result of this twice-a-year Herculean effort is that our teachers become physically and mentally drained after another furious round of conferences. Both teachers and parents feel rushed to communicate everything they want to share with each other. But in one area of the building, I observed a relaxed teacher walking about her room, listening to her students talk to their parents about their learning thus far. Several students were in the classroom at the same time, leading the parents in a discussion of their work. The teacher herself was more of an observer and greeter. As they exited the room, both parents and students made it a point to tell me how impressed they were with this "new" way of conferencing.

Although we have seen great results from student-led conferences, there are disadvantages. Many parents really enjoy this concept, yet still ask for a "traditional" conference in which they can meet with the teacher privately to hear his or her professional viewpoint regarding their child's abilities and progress. In such cases, of course, this requires more, not less, effort on the part of the teacher. However, I feel that student-led conferencing has a great deal of merit, and I wanted the rest of my staff to consider the perspective of one teacher who had experienced much success in getting students to take ownership of their own education.

Friday Focus!

October 22

"When the mind is thinking, it is talking to itself." Plato

Believe it or not, before too long we will approach the holiday season. Some of us already have a gift list that we are compiling. However, have you thought about the greatest gift you can give to our students? I challenge you to empower them with the ability to participate in the assessment of their own work. Jean Kerr Stenmark (1991) believed that one of the greatest gifts students can receive is the capability and willingness to assess their own progress and learning. Involve your students in their ability to analyze their thinking processes.

Guide your students' development of metacognitive strategies by asking questions that make them reflect upon their means of thinking. The process of reporting and conferencing is changing from a teacher-directed exercise to a collaborative, ongoing process designed to support learning. Student-led conferencing does not take place only during the early-release days. Students are participating in an ongoing process of reflecting and improving upon their skills throughout the year. Allowing your students to lead their own conferences promotes the following:

- Students take a lead role.
- Work samples or demonstrations are used to show proof of learning.
- Students invite an audience to participate in the process.
- Audiences take an active role and give specific feedback to the learner.
- Ultimately, your students become assessors and thinkers about their own work.

As you relax and begin to refocus on the second part of this semester, reflect upon what role you would like your students to play in the assessment process. Please listen to what David (one of our own students) has to say about the effect of student-led conferences upon his ability to learn.

David and his mother exit the classroom. They are both beaming. He quickly states to his teacher, "That was the first time that I've ever been able to really discuss my work with my mom. Most of the time I have sat in a chair outside in the hallway while the teachers talked about me behind the door. This time, I was doing the talking. Some of what I told my mom was ways that I had improved. I also told her the things that I needed to improve on and how I planned to do that. I am the one who can change that, and she and I both know how that is going to be done."

Give your students this gift—the ability to take the lead in assessing their work by leading their own student-led conference.

Happy Weekend!

Cathy

12

Teacher Observations

Throughout my career as a school administrator, my number one priority has been visibility within the school, particularly in classrooms. My own experience as a classroom teacher is one reason I place such an emphasis on administrator visibility. Too often, I taught at schools in which I could go for an entire school year without a classroom visit from the principal. At one high school in which I taught, my students did not know the name of the principal. If the principal truly is the instructional leader of the school, he or she must spend the majority of the time where instruction occurs—in classrooms.

Who benefits when an administrator visits a classroom? In my opinion, the teacher, the students, and the administrator all benefit. As an elementary school administrator, my goal was to—at the very minimum—step foot into every classroom every day. At the middle school level, I visit every classroom twice a week. Even as a high school administrator, I managed to visit every classroom at an extremely large campus at least once a week. Frequent administrative visits to classrooms send a powerful message to both teachers and students. Our very best teachers appreciate that we care enough about what they do to visit regularly. For our mediocre teachers, administrative visits are equally important. We can gain firsthand information in order to help these teachers improve or, when necessary, to document evidence for dismissal. Much like our best teachers, our best students also appreciate a principal who is in their classrooms regularly. They enjoy sharing what it is they are doing in their classrooms. If both our best teachers and our best students think it is a good idea for administrators to be in classrooms, then it is very likely indeed that this is a good idea.

I firmly believe that there is little I do in my office that cannot be done in the classroom. As a result, everything I do that can possibly be completed in a classroom is done there as opposed to in my office. Tasks I complete in classrooms include reviewing and signing timesheets for classified staff, writing positive notes to teachers, planning agendas for future meetings, and reading and sorting my mail. Of course, certain tasks are best completed in my office, including hiring personnel, conferencing with teachers, and composing and responding to e-mails. These are tasks that I focus on before and after school. During the school hours, I arrange my work schedule so that I am completing work that can be accomplished outside of my office. Students appreciate seeing principals working in the classrooms; it lets them know that—like them—there are many assignments that I must complete each day. Our best teachers always enjoy another adult in the classroom as well. While I am completing my work, I can also monitor student behavior and student learning. Kids tend to perform even better than normal when I am working alongside them.

Another benefit of regular, albeit brief, classroom visits is that they make official and lengthier teacher observations much less intrusive and much more comfortable for the teacher, the administrator, and the students. If I have already visited a classroom 20 or so times before sitting in for an extended observation, sometimes the students barely notice I'm there. The teacher, too, is much more relaxed and natural, and I have a better sense of what to expect in the way of the teaching and learning I will see. As I begin my formal observations, I try to focus on three main areas of teaching, all of which directly affect the amount of learning that will occur.

Designing, Managing, Monitoring

My formal observations are unannounced, unscheduled visits that last anywhere from 45 to 60 minutes. Since I have already been to each classroom many times prior to this, there is no reason to schedule a visit to observe a lesson that has been planned just for this occasion. During my visit, I try to find evidence that supports our goal for teachers to *design* engaging, quality work assignments; *manage* the learning environment; and *monitor* student learning throughout the lesson.

In a sense, I am really observing students more than teachers when supervising and evaluating classroom instruction. After all, what I am really interested in is what the students are learning as a result of the instruction that has occurred. As I conduct these observations, I typically sit quietly and jot notes to myself, but if it is appropriate, I will move about the room and talk quietly with students. The most common question I ask of them is, "What are you learning?" Often, their responses are as telling as anything I observe on my own. In the classrooms of our very best teachers, the students are quite adept at explaining in detail just what it is they are doing and what they have been working on up to this point. They can also tell me with precision any procedures in place for the classroom, ranging from what type of writing utensil to use, to how and when to ask a question, to whether or not it is acceptable to ask to use the restroom. Great teachers clearly outline expectations regarding all areas of their classroom and practice getting students to meet these expectations daily. By the time I conduct my formal observation, exemplary behavior and performance is already second nature to students learning from great teachers.

Formal observations afford me the opportunity to revisit one of my core values regarding instruction, which is that we should aim for effective, efficient, and relevant lessons. Within 24 hours of conducting a formal observation, I place a written narrative of what I observed in the teacher's mailbox. I close each narrative by asking if, in the opinion of the teacher, the lesson was effective, efficient, and relevant, along with the question, "Why or why not?" Typically, our best teachers are much more critical of themselves in this area than I.

Ideally, administrators and teachers should sit down several times a year to discuss past performance and future goals for improvement. Yet in a large school, this is not always realistic. Again, I find that the best way to stay on top of what is going on in individual classrooms is through frequent brief visits along with an occasional extended observation.

The 12th Friday

Typically, October is the month in which I am finally prepared to make extended visits to each teacher's classroom. I wanted to let all teachers know two things at this point: things I had been observing that were extremely positive, and what I would be looking for as I visited other classrooms. Although I follow our school system's guidelines in observing and evaluating our teaching staff, I bring many of my own ideas to this process as well.

This week's Friday Focus began with a quotation exhorting our teachers to examine what is taught, why it is taught, and what mastery looks like. This quote is a perfect reminder of messages we send throughout the year to our teachers. In revisiting the concepts of effectiveness and efficiency, I suggest that effectiveness might be looked at as "doing the right things," and efficiency can be thought of as "doing things right." Our very best teachers do both each and every day. The observation process is primarily a time to affirm these behaviors in the vast majority of our teachers and to stress the idea of continuous improvement for all, regardless of our current level of proficiency.

In the following Friday Focus, I offered several specific ways to enhance instruction; however, the overall intent was to provide a consistent focus for the entire school in terms of what effective teachers do in their classrooms each day. Although teachers should enjoy a great amount of autonomy in how they conduct their classes, what is to be taught and how we assess what is learned should remain consistent from teacher to teacher within each common grade level and subject area. The information shared below is applicable to all teachers at any school.

Friday Focus!

October 29

To provide a knowledge-centered classroom environment, attention must be given to what is taught, why it is taught, and what competence or mastery looks like.
(Bransford, Brown, & Cocking, 2000, p. 24)

Since the beginning of this month, I have conducted an extended observation (45 minutes or longer) in one classroom each day, in addition to brief drop-in visits throughout the building. Immediately after an extended observation, I return to my office and type up a fairly lengthy report of what I observed. I typically provide written responses under three headings:

- The teacher designs quality knowledge work that actively engages students in learning.
- The teacher manages time, people, space, assessment data, and technology.
- The teacher monitors and adapts the work provided to achieve desired results.

Following these sections, I include a "Questions/Comments" section. The final questions I ask within this category are always the following: "Was this lesson effective, efficient, and relevant? Why or why not?"

My focus during these observations is not evaluative, but supervisory. The goal of supervision is for teachers to analyze their own teaching while in the act of teaching by measuring its effectiveness, efficiency, and relevancy and making the necessary adjustments (Rice & Taylor, 2000). To determine effectiveness, ask yourself, "Did students master the skills taught?" To gauge efficiency, ask, "How long does it take for the student to master the skills taught?" As for relevance, ask, "Is the learning meaningful? Can students apply it?" The beginning of a lesson is sometimes referred to as the "set." Three things you can do to make the set effective, efficient, and relevant include involving the students, establishing relevance by relating the learning to students' life experiences, and making a statement of learning. We typically end our lessons with some form of closure. Three things you can do during closure to help make the lesson effective, efficient, and relevant include involving the students, restating the learning, and identifying the critical elements or the important parts of the learning.

Another way of mulling over the concepts of effectiveness and efficiency is to consider effectiveness as doing the right things, and efficiency as doing things right. That is, we must ascertain precisely what key skills our students need to learn. Then, we must set about teaching them in a logical, orderly manner. As for relevance, I have read a great deal of research that suggests that the most powerful principle of learning is meaning. At OMS, our teachers are masters of making learning meaningful. While observing in classrooms, I focus on students as often as I focus on teachers. In so doing, I rarely detect students mired in ennui. For example, like most outstanding social studies teachers, Melissa Sessa uses lecturing as one teaching technique. However, unlike teachers elsewhere, Melissa's lectures are more like stories; she indubitably imparts the exact same information being taught through lectures at other schools, but in a way that is much more meaningful to students. I doubt that her students even realize she is "lecturing."

My hope is that we regularly remind ourselves to assess whether or not our lessons are effective, efficient, and relevant. As you know, all students can learn, though not at the same rate, or at the same level, or in the same way. Our job is to closely monitor our own teaching and to make the necessary adjustments while in the act of teaching so that all learners are learning and mastering key concepts. Thanks for providing learning opportunities for our students that are effective, efficient, and relevant. *More importantly, thanks for* Teaching with Passion *each day!*

Have a great weekend!

Jeff

13

Learning How to Learn

For this week's Friday Focus, one of our most respected teacher leaders wrote on a topic that is near and dear to her heart and that had been a professional development training focus at our school prior to my arrival. The topic of her Friday Focus dovetailed nicely with the previous week's, in which I shared some strategies for effective teaching as I continued my extended classroom observations. This writing also addresses key elements of teaching and learning and serves as a powerful reminder of concepts most of the teachers had learned in earlier training sessions.

In a word, this week's topic is about metacognition, or thinking about thinking. The author encourages teachers to take their teaching one step further by getting their students to understand their own thinking and cognitive processes.

CRISS

Prior to my tenure as principal of our school, the entire staff had undergone extensive training in something known as CRISS, which stands for **C**reating **I**ndependence for **S**tudent-Owned **S**trategies (Project CRISS, 2005). Many of our current teachers had undergone this training and were familiar with the tenets reinforced below. The author of this week's Friday Focus had taken an avid interest in the CRISS philosophy and had been instrumental in encouraging other teachers in our system to incorporate the ideas into daily classroom practice.

The goal behind the CRISS initiative is to get students to better organize, understand, and retain course information. The philosophy behind CRISS begins with the belief that most students truly do not know how to learn (Project CRISS, 2005). They approach their learning haphazardly, relying on innate abilities and teacher input. With such an approach, our most intelligent students will get by on their natural strengths but still may fail to deeply learn and understand essential content. Our struggling students, meanwhile, may get left behind altogether as they move into high school and beyond. CRISS encourages teachers to show students how to learn by modeling, demonstrating, and explaining each new big idea being taught.

The 13th Friday

Beth Richardson, this week's author, teaches computer literacy. Mrs. Richardson is not only one of the finest classroom teachers I have ever known, she is also one of the most valuable leaders in our school system. She even left the classroom for one year to serve as a school administrator, but quickly returned to her true passion, classroom teaching.

Beth is an expert on the CRISS philosophy and principles, having served as a CRISS trainer. She wrote eloquently about her passionate belief in these learning strategies. As had become the norm for our school's Friday Focus teachings, Beth began with quotations, one of which she attributed to an ancient Chinese proverb, and the other to herself! She closed her Friday Focus with her regular and unique sign-off and even attached a "Key Elements of Learning" handout for our teachers, along with directions for inexpensively enlarging the handout to poster size for classroom display. The Friday Focus stood as an effective reminder to other teachers that training kids in metacognitive ways will enrich their learning.

Friday Focus!

November 5

"Give a man a fish and he will eat for a day. Teach a man to fish and he will eat for the rest of his life." Ancient Chinese proverb

"Teach a child content and he will pass a test. Teach a child HOW to learn all content and he will pass ALL tests." Beth Richardson

A good teacher teaches students how to become their own teacher. Remember that the highest level of learning is evidenced by being able to teach someone else. This is why some kids and adults are successful and some aren't. Some know how to teach themselves (learn) whatever needs to be learned; others don't have that skill.

You and I share a great and honorable mission in life. We are here on the planet to help people "learn how to learn" and, in effect, become teachers. Now, I know all of our students aren't going to major in education, but can you honestly say that as an adult they will live even *one* day without having to be "the teacher" in some way for themselves, their own children, their colleagues, their family, or their friends?

Do you remember these?

- Prior knowledge
- Defined purpose

- Active learning
  - Active reading
  - Discussion
  - Writing
- Reorganization
- Metacognition

Some of you are saying, "Oh no, here she goes again on her CRISS soapbox." Yes, they have something to do with **CRISS** (**C**reating **I**ndependence for **S**tudent-Owned **S**trategies).

The list above spells out the key elements of learning (Project CRISS, 2005). These are elements that need to be present in a good learning or studying activity if you want the information to stick in the brain. Think of them as the solid foundation for real learning—learning that stays with a person and can be recalled when needed.

As teachers, we deliver the knowledge. At OMS we usually dispense the knowledge to our students in a fancy package or "learning strategy." Many of us use time-proven CRISS strategies and strategies from other reputable, reliable sources.

However, the light bulb moment for me (and I mean the light bulbs they use in the major league sports arenas) occurred when the CRISS trainer said that *our job is only **half-done** when we use these great strategies in our lessons each day.* Really, my mouth was hanging open. How dare she? What did she mean, half-done? I researched, planned, prepped, and delivered with glorious flair. What did she mean, half-done? What more could I do? I couldn't *pour it into their brains!!!*

But then the trainer explained. After using a strategy with the kids, we must *communicate* to the students *why* we chose that strategy and point out the areas it hit in the Key Elements of Learning chart. We then have to encourage the students to think about how it worked for them (this is metacognition, or thinking about your own thinking).

To me, this is the *missing piece* in education today. This is why I got so excited when it finally clicked in my brain (as I, an 18-year veteran teacher, was sitting through a CRISS class for the third time on my way to becoming a CRISS trainer). We are teaching our hearts out delivering the content, but what we are forgetting is teaching them *how to learn* the content. Some of our brightest students are making all As, but they are not learning how to learn material when it becomes challenging. (I wish someone had taught me how to learn and study before I went to college.)

Guide the students in asking themselves the following questions:

☐ Did I make the grade I wanted?

☐ Did the learning stick? Will I really remember this six months or a year from now?

☐ Do I need to do something else for myself to make the knowledge stick?

☐ Could I use this strategy myself at home (even if the teacher didn't tell me to do it) when studying for a social studies test? Science test? French test?

Ask the students these questions:

☐ Are you studying at home but then not doing as well on the test as you would like?

☐ Do you know what to do for yourself at home when the teacher doesn't give a specific assignment but just says to study your notes?

☐ What are some of the things we do in class that really help you to remember material?

After discussing the answers to these questions, encourage students to do something that hits several areas on the Key Elements of Learning list: talk about what they learned with someone, reorganize it a different way, make a visual organizer, and so on. Remember, it's a good learning or studying strategy if it hits several of the elements on the list, but it certainly doesn't have to include all the elements at one time.

To me, this is teaching students how to be lifelong learners! This is teaching them how to learn anything that comes their way in the next 50 years, some of which we can't even imagine. This is what it means to be a *teacher*—not a deliverer of facts, but someone who *shows them the way* no matter what a future teacher or boss (good or bad) throws out to them.

How many of us have our Key Elements of Learning chart still up on our wall so that we can refer to it often, showing the students the *how* and *why* of what we are doing and *what they should be doing for themselves at home when it is study time?* I'm embarrassed to say that I went the whole first nine weeks without mine, but I put it back up this week.

Please take the extra five or even 10 minutes to address the how and why you "do it this way" with your students. Don't think of it as losing time for content. Think of it as giving them a better future—a way to survive without you. You will be bestowing on them a gift far greater than a high score on a standardized test (which, for the record, will improve anyway with this approach). You will be giving them the gift of *how* to learn and teach themselves the unbelievable amount of content that awaits them in the future. You will be fulfilling your great and honorable mission in its highest form.

Thanks for all you do to make this the best place I have ever worked! Be blessed as you bless the future.

Love and light,   ·

Beth

P.S. The attachment can be made into a really big poster at Office Max for less than $5. Come see mine if you want to see what it will look like!

14

Teaching: Art or Science?

In one of my very first graduate classes, the professor engaged us in a debate as to whether effective teaching is first and foremost an art or a science. Of course, the answer is both, and our most brilliant teachers have mastered the artistic as well as the scientific components of their noble profession. While both are essential to the success of any teacher, I still feel that most teachers, including our very best ones, lean ever-so-slightly toward one of the two. At our own school, for instance, I often brag about the educational training our staff has gained. Yet, if I had to choose, I would say that what sets our teachers apart and makes us unique is that we emphasize what constitutes the "art" of teaching just a tad more than the "science" of teaching.

The 14th Friday

Harry Wong is well known to nearly all educators and is the perfect source to look to in gaining insights into both the art and the science of teaching. While no one can dispute Wong's research-based writings on effective teaching, most of us familiar with his work and philosophy would agree that—at first glance—he is more artist than scientist. The quote excerpted from his masterpiece text, which opens this Friday Focus, reinforces that assumption. Yet the subtitle to his most famous work (Wong & Wong, 1998) is *How to Be an Effective Teacher.* Certainly, this conjures up the idea of the science behind our craft.

In the following Friday Focus, I shared with teachers six traits commonly possessed by exemplary teachers. Interestingly, three of these strike me more as "scientific" components, while the other three strike me as "artistic" skills. The sixth trait listed, instructional skills, is one that I broke down further into five key areas for our teachers to consider as the "science" of effective teaching. In other words, what must any teacher do in order to create and deliver an effective lesson?

At the time of this writing, I was still in the middle of conducting extended classroom observations, and I once again wanted to promote active thinking among our staff about what good teaching and good lessons look like. While most of the research I shared in the Friday Focus had been around for decades, the findings were tried and true and represented some of the constants in an ever-changing profession.

In the final paragraph of the Friday Focus, I highlighted two more teachers at our school, one who clearly exhibits on a daily basis the concept of the teacher as artist, and another who is the epitome of the teacher as scientist. Throughout the year, we made it a point to recognize individual teachers within the Friday Focus who live the theme of that week's topic throughout the year. For this week, in selecting two teachers at our school, I recognized a 27-year veteran teacher along with one of our first-year teachers. Both are outstanding, and both are proficient in the art, as well as the science, of teaching.

Friday Focus!

November 12

When you look at the truly effective teachers, you will also find caring, warm, lovable people. Years later, when the students remember their most significant teachers, the ones that they remember the most are the ones who really cared about them. Effective teachers know that they cannot get a student to learn unless that student knows that the teacher cares. (Wong & Wong, 1998)

Quotes like the one above from Wong and Wong relate to the art of teaching more than the science of teaching. This remains my primary passion related to education: the "artistic" abilities necessary to become and remain an outstanding educator and living "The Otwell Way" by caring deeply for our students and our craft. However, it is important to note that the subtitle to Wong and Wong's now-famous tome, *The First Days of School*, is *How to Be an Effective Teacher.* Although the *art* of teaching is my own primary area of interest, one which goes a long way toward making one an effective teacher, we must also examine the *science* of teaching—focusing on research that sheds light on what makes some teachers more effective, efficient, and relevant than other teachers. In one of the first graduate classes I ever took, I learned that teachers who were identified as exemplary possessed six common characteristics (Rice & Taylor, 2000):

- Knowledge of content
- Planning skills

- Use, after selection, of appropriate materials
- Classroom management skills
- Human relations skills
- Instructional skills

Obviously, the qualities listed above are neither esoteric, mystical, nor new. In addition, all but one is necessary for success in any line of work, not just teaching. The one characteristic unique to the teaching profession is instructional skills. What exactly are "instructional skills"? Rice and Taylor (2000) identified these five core instructional skills:

- Selecting an objective at or near the correct range of difficulty and level of complexity
- Teaching to the objective
- Maintaining the focus of the learner on the objective
- Using, without abusing, the principles of learning
- Monitoring and adjusting

(As a mnemonic device for my exam, I used the acronym TUMMS to recall these five instructional practices.) *The science of teaching, then, comprises these five instructional skills.* No matter what subject or grade, these skills remain constant. Both the kindergarten teacher and the algebra teacher must select objectives at or near the correct range of difficulty and level of complexity. Elementary and secondary teachers need to teach the objectives while maintaining the focus of the learners on those objectives. The principles of learning are present in any instructional lesson, and all effective teachers monitor and adjust their lessons as situations arise.

An oft-debated topic in many of my education classes revolved around whether effective teaching is an art or a science. Personally, I have always focused more on the art of teaching than the science of teaching. However, in reality, the two are equally important as well as interrelated. Many of us at Otwell Middle School are artists at the craft of teaching. To watch Joanie Anderton in action, for example, is akin to viewing a performer worthy of acclaim. Meanwhile, Frank McCormack is not only a scientist (literally), he is also well versed in the scientific principles of effective teaching. Even the most sterling teaching performance may prove meaningless unless such a performance is based upon a sound scientific knowledge base. At the same time, the most scientifically sound lesson in the history of pedagogy will prove fruitless in terms of student learning if the teacher is not proficient in the art of teaching. Because OMS is staffed by teachers who are both artists and scientists, we are able to *Teach with Passion* each day.

Happy Weekend!

Jeff

15

Giving Thanks

The 15th Friday

The following Friday Focus was sent out to all staff on the Friday before Thanksgiving week. As we would only have two days of school the following week, I wanted to veer from the usual pattern of sharing instructional strategies or educational philosophies and simply thank our teachers for all that they did to improve our school each day.

The overall tone of the writing is humorous, yet sincere. Whenever appropriate, I like to share self-deprecating personal anecdotes about my own adolescent years. Relating a story regarding my enthusiasm for '70s rocker Peter Frampton seemed a fun way to begin this writing. Yet the other quote I shared was more appropriate still—certainly at our school, but more importantly, at every school in existence. There is no successful school without successful people working in it. The finest educational programs available to us cannot make us successful unless we have successful people implementing them. Technology has certainly changed the way we conduct our core business, yet our profession is one that will always remain a "people business" first and foremost, from the secretaries who greet visitors, to the cafeteria workers who serve us food, to the custodians who keep our facility clean, to the teachers who make our students' days. During this time of giving thanks, I wanted to let all of these folks know how much they were appreciated.

Although I brag often and loudly about our teaching staff, I spend less time publicly praising our administrative team. This writing was a great opportunity to praise and thank them for all the work they do in leading our students and teachers successfully each day. Our school is located in a bustling suburban community that is ever-changing and growing rapidly. The school mirrors our community in terms of this change and growth. Working in one of the fastest-growing counties in the nation means that we are faced with change on a yearly, if not daily, basis. We believe that while such change can bring challenges, it also creates opportunities. Each year at our school we say goodbye to departing staff and welcome new teachers into our family. We often talk about "The Otwell Way," as referenced below, yet our administrative team works hard to balance what it is we want in hiring new teachers at our school. Of course, we want to train them in how we currently teach and learn at our school. We hope they will embrace the core values that we hold near and dear to our hearts. Yet part of "The Otwell Way," ironically, is knowing that our way is not necessarily the only or best way to do things. We are constantly striving for improvement; learning from our new teachers is one way we can improve our school.

As principal, I spend a great deal of time reviewing safety plans, scrutinizing curriculum standards and materials, attending meetings, responding to phone calls and e-mails, and performing countless other tasks. Just as important as all of these—if not more so—is making the time to thank our staff for all that they do.

Friday Focus!

November 19

When asked to identify what made the school so good, every person, without fail, said it was the people of the school: the children, the families, and, most importantly, the staff. Nobody said, "We have a really great computer lab" or "a brand-new reading textbook."
(Eaker, DuFour, & DuFour, 2002)

"Thank YOU!" (Peter Frampton, circa 1976, introducing the song, "Baby I Love Your Way" on the Frampton Comes Alive album)

Many of you are probably too young to even remember Frampton's classic live album (on the other hand, Suzanne and a few select others may, of course, be a tad too old); as for myself, I do vaguely recall spending a significant portion of my junior year of high school listening to Frampton and thinking he was really cool. My knuckleheaded buddies and I would even imitate his seemingly forgettable, "Thank YOU!" whenever the opportunity presented itself. With the Thanksgiving holidays swiftly approaching, I thought it a felicitous time to deviate slightly from the typical themes of our weekly Friday Focus and simply offer heartfelt thanks to all of you for enriching the lives of our students and me.

I'm deeply thankful for our administrative team at Otwell. In many ways, their individual and collective greatness mirrors that of our overall staff. We have a returning veteran administrator in Scott Feldkamp. With several years of experience as an assistant principal at OMS, Scott possesses valuable expertise and insights that help us all. Scott offers consistently sound advice and judgment; his organizational skills and meticulous attention to details are unsurpassed. In Van Lewsader, we have an administrator who is changing roles at OMS just this year, moving from classroom teacher to administrator extraordinaire. Van's amazing ability to multitask as athletic director, test coordinator, in-school suspension coordinator, and 7th grade disciplinarian never ceases to astound me. Finally, in Suzanne Korngold, we have an administrator who is brand-new to Otwell. Suzanne has made an immediate positive impact on our entire school community with her compassion, her intellect, and her overall commitment to excellence. In my short reign as principal at OMS, I can confidently state that I have made at least one outstanding decision: bringing Suzanne on board to take over from the nearly irreplaceable Dawn Melin. Scott, Van, and Suzanne are tireless workers and trusted friends, and I am deeply thankful that they are here each day supporting our teachers and students.

Our entire staff nicely parallels our administrative team: while in Scott, we have a returning assistant principal, we also have many returning veteran teachers and support staff on whom we rely for their wisdom and for sharing and spreading "The Otwell Way." We also have teachers who are returning, yet (like Van) are in new roles this year. We applaud you for your flexibility and willingness to accept new challenges that benefit our kids. Finally, we have a solid core of teachers completely new to Otwell this year. Each of them (like Suzanne) has brought with them a multitude of skills and traits that are helping us all to grow continuously as professionals.

Whether you are a returning teacher, a teacher in a new role, or a teacher new to OMS, I am sincerely thankful that you are here. I have the best job in the world because I am surrounded by the best teachers in the world. In the above quote, Eaker and colleagues have clearly stated what makes our own school great: it is not our pristine facility, or our world-class curriculum, or our many extracurricular offerings; instead, it is each of you performing great deeds day in and day out. As Peter Frampton said, "Thank YOU!" for teaching me so clearly what effective teachers do differently, and thanks for *Teaching with Passion* each day!

Have a great weekend!

Jeff

16

In the Middle

I have had the good fortune to spend 10 years working at the middle school level. In addition, I have enjoyed six or more years' service at both the elementary and high school levels. All three levels are unique and seem to have their own distinct advantages and challenges for educators and students alike. At the elementary level, many of my friends enjoy the fact that their students are still so excited about coming to school. My friends at the high school level seem to enjoy being able to pass along their love of a certain academic discipline to their students. At the middle school level, we truly are a bridge between the two. While no one level of teaching is any easier or more difficult than another, students at each level arrive with vastly different abilities and needs.

People and Programs

It is a good idea for administrators at all levels to periodically remind teachers of the special characteristics and needs of the young people who attend our schools. While the following Friday Focus pertains to those of us at the middle grades level, one could just as easily be written and geared for elementary or high school educators. At the middle school level, we have a national organization, the National Middle School Association (NMSA), which specifically works on behalf of middle school students by supporting and educating those who work with them on a daily basis.

At the time of this writing, I was finishing up work on my dissertation, in which I had exhaustively researched the history and philosophy of middle grades education. The NMSA has identified 14 cultural and programmatic characteristics of successful middle schools. These cultural characteristics neatly align with our people skills, while the programmatic traits, obviously, relate to our programs. At our school, we agree with Whitaker (2002) and Eaker, DuFour, and DuFour (2002) that it is our people, not our programs, that make us effective, yet we understand the value and necessity of solid instructional and extracurricular programs.

While we work closely with both our elementary and high school neighbors to ensure smooth transitions at both ends of our "bridge," it is important that we always remember that we truly are in the middle. Although we ease and nurture our incoming sixth graders into the middle school world at one end and prepare our eighth graders for high school at the other end, our true purpose is to look neither too far behind nor too far ahead. Instead, we focus on the developmental, social, emotional, and academic needs of kids ranging in age from 10 to 15 and work hard to instill in them a love for learning. Many of the programmatic and cultural characteristics of successful middle schools, as outlined by the NMSA, are reminiscent of past and future Friday Focus themes. They serve as a reminder to our teachers about what our students need us to do and provide in order for them to succeed.

The 16th Friday

Obviously, everyone working at our school is familiar with and has chosen to work with middle grades learners. Yet, at times, we forget that our students are at what can be a very difficult time in their young lives. In reviewing what it is that our national organization indicates constitutes successful middle schools, I wanted teachers to both rejoice in those tasks that we obviously do so well and focus on, perhaps, those few that merited our attention as areas needing improvement.

In this Friday Focus, I recounted a conversation with one of our very finest and most veteran teachers—and one of the few on staff more senior in age than myself. In praising her many characteristics I reiterated why our staff admires her so much. I also used this opportunity to highlight several individual teachers at our school and suggest that while they would succeed as teachers at any grade level, not every great teacher can succeed at the middle grades level. To paraphrase Charles Dickens, teaching "in the middle" can be the best of times *and* the worst of times.

Friday Focus!

November 26

Every day, twenty million diverse, rapidly changing 10- to 15-year olds enrolled in our nation's middle level schools are making critical and complex life choices. They are forming the attitudes, values, and habits of mind that will largely direct their behavior as adults. They deserve schools that support them fully during this key phase of life. (National Middle School Association, 1995)

Although nine of my teaching years in public education have occurred at the middle school level, my most recent experience prior to arriving at Otwell Middle School was at the high school and elementary school levels. Upon being named principal of OMS, I immediately began reacclimating myself to all things middle school (belching, the hilarity of passing gas, grabbing/poking/prodding, etc.). As I began my dissertation work, I spent even more time scrutinizing middle schools, researching the history of the middle school movement, the philosophy of the middle school concept, and the developmental needs of middle grades learners. I began spending an inordinate amount of time surfing the National Middle School Association (NMSA) website (http://www.nmsa.org). Although I felt knowledgeable about middle grades education and middle grades students, I learned a great deal about what our national organization views as quality people and program characteristics for the middle grades. As middle school practitioners immersed "in the middle," you may be like me in thinking that we are already pretty darn familiar with the whole middle school deal, and you would be correct. But it is worthwhile, in my opinion, to revisit what our national organization believes is of paramount importance to the success of our middle schools.

As middle school teachers, it would behoove us all to at least be familiar with the NMSA position paper, *This We Believe* (1995). In this publication, the NMSA outlines 14 characteristics of successful middle schools, eight of which pertain to school culture and six of which relate to programmatic characteristics. Whether you have seen these before or are learning about them for the first time, I hope you will scan these attributes of successful schools. Are they indeed important? Are we adhering to these tenets at OMS? Where do we rate on each of the following? Are we an obvious "10" on any one of the below? Are we terribly deficient in another? Are we working on any of these during the current school year?

Cultural Characteristics

- *Educators who value working with this age group* and are prepared to do so
- Courageous, *collaborative* leadership
- A *shared vision* that guides decisions
- An *inviting*, supportive, and safe environment
- *High expectations* for every member of the learning community
- Students and teachers *engaged in active learning*
- An *adult advocate* for every student
- School-initiated *family and community partnerships*

Programmatic Characteristics

- Curriculum that is *relevant, challenging,* integrative, and exploratory

- *Multiple learning and teaching approaches* that respond to young adolescents' diversity

- *Assessment and evaluation programs that promote quality learning*

- Organizational structures that support *meaningful relationships* and learning

- Schoolwide efforts and policies that foster health, wellness, and *safety*

- *Multifaceted guidance and support services*

How did we do? Any "10s"? (Perhaps we get the highest ranking in "educators who value working with this age group and are prepared to do so.") Are there any we are working on this year (maybe "a shared vision that guides decisions")? Any that we really have not addressed adequately and are again unprepared to do so this year?

My good friend and esteemed colleague, Janet Vanderhoff, is one of my heroes. I admire her greatly and marvel at her enthusiasm, energy, and willingness to experiment. In a recent conversation around the microwave, Janet chided me about my competitiveness. I pled guilty as charged, especially when it comes to our wonderful school. Do I want us to be the best middle school anywhere? Indeed, I do. Are we? If not, I'd like to visit the one that is. Can we rest on our laurels? As you all know, we cannot. Rather, we must continually examine what it is we do. Often, we find that what we do far surpasses what any other school does. At other times, we may want to focus on what we can do even better. What makes a great middle school according to the NMSA may not be the final word in effective middle schools. On the other hand, the organization's list merits our attention as professional middle school educators.

During new teacher orientation this year, I stated to our new folks my long-standing belief that ours is the hardest job of any in education. The challenges facing us at the middle school level are profound in comparison to those facing our elementary and high school colleagues. Yet I think our rewards are greater as well. Janet Vanderhoff, Karen Pigott, Ronnie McNeese, Phil Westray, Doris Dickerson, Tom Long, and Pam Poe could all walk across the street tomorrow and immediately be effective high school teachers, as could nearly all OMS teachers. Is the reverse scenario as likely?

Having experienced both levels, I would hazard a guess in the negative. Thank you for taking the time to remind yourselves what middle school is all about. More importantly, thank you for choosing to teach at the middle school level, the noblest pursuit of all and the level at which *Teaching with Passion* each day is a must!

Happy Weekend!

Jeff

17

K.I.S.S.

As a young boy, I was a master at taking the simple and making it complicated. As a result, it was my father who first introduced me to K.I.S.S., as he regularly implored me to "Keep it simple, Stupid." While we can leave off the "Stupid" part, perhaps, "keeping it simple" is often a good approach for both students and teachers to bear in mind as we go about our core business of teaching and learning.

When I was in seventh grade myself, I tackled "Can Man Live on the Moon?" as a science fair theme. My shrewd father immediately realized my intellectual capabilities were not up to the task of ascertaining whether or not it would be feasible to establish permanent residence on the moon, and he suggested instead that I investigate something I could actually understand. Being a seventh grader, I refused. Although I learned nothing about the plausibility of residing on the moon and conducted no scientific research, I did make a really neat art project representing the lunar surface. Many years later, when I was teaching seventh grade and coaching the boys' basketball team, I was still looking for ways to complicate matters. On my basketball team was an extraordinarily tall and talented young man who currently plays professional basketball. Although a fine young man, he was often getting into minor trouble with his other teachers. I concocted an elaborate system for keeping his behavior in check and shared my plan with my principal. My principal shrewdly replied, "Jeff, he's not that sophisticated. Just tell him what to do and make him do it."

Keeping it simple is one of my favorite mantras as I go about the job of working with teachers and students. It is not unlike another of my favorite refrains: less is more. I know that for my own learning style, the less you tell me, the more I take in. Our students have a similar attention span, it would appear. While it is always prudent to overplan our instruction, we should remember that it is not imperative to "cover" it all. It is much more valuable to learn a limited amount of information and learn it well than to "cover" a huge amount of complicated subject matter.

The 17th Friday

Robin Sellen is an extraordinary math teacher and the author of the following Friday Focus. Robin is a very unique human being who describes herself as a former hippie. She has a heart of gold and an uncanny ability to reach even our most at-risk students. Although she is certified and highly qualified to teach a wide variety of subjects, she chooses to work with students who need extra support in math.

Robin is quite clearly an ardent supporter of the K.I.S.S. philosophy. She juxtaposed language from an actual mathematics curriculum resource text with well-known, everyday phrases as evidence in support of her perspective. In her Friday Focus, Robin practiced what she preaches by offering a very short and direct writing. In it, she used the terms "lasting knowledge" and "enduring success." These are crucial to our core business of student learning. Too often, we feel that we must do more, more, and more in an era of accountability, high-stakes testing, and a standards-based curriculum. While I find it highly laudable that we hold ourselves accountable for student achievement, we must remember that the key is not more of the same, but a smarter approach. Oftentimes a succinct and simple style is just that.

Friday Focus!

December 3

Delusion, Distraction, Waste

The preface of a mathematics resource book informs the reader of the following:

In accordance with our principle of relative inclusiveness, we have attempted to define every term used in our definitions. However, just as we have tried to set the level of each entry for the reader who is likely to have recourse to it, so we have only explicitly signaled a cross-reference where we judge it likely to assist that reader, and for synonymous terms we have attempted to cross-refer the less common to the more common, although a degree of arbitrariness (to say nothing of subjectivity) is inevitable in such judgments.
(Borowski & Borwein, 2002)

Such a paragraph may bring to mind some of the following:

"Where's the beef?" (An advertising firm's well-deserved $20 million)

"Separate the wheat from the chaff." (A Biblical caution)

"Focus on the substance of the idea."
(Found in every language arts text)

"Get to the point." (Request of a dominant left-brained person to a dominant right-brained one)

"Clear as mud." (A disturbing literary mental picture)

All the authors wanted the reader to know in the above excerpt is that they had chosen the terms they thought were the most essential for student learning and tried to make them easy to understand. Why did they have to do all of the colorful packaging? Well, perhaps their love of the English language clouded their understanding of their readers' needs and interest level. As teachers, our interests and love of particular topics can do this to us—and our students—as well. In the classroom, and in our daily lives, "keeping it simple" by focusing on the substance of things can make life easier. However, we shouldn't confuse "keeping it simple" with "making it easy." Challenging, interesting, thought-provoking lessons are still possible, but delusion, distraction, and waste will interfere with the lasting knowledge we are striving to impart to our kids.

Our lives, as teachers, are now considered among the top three stress-producing jobs in the world. So here is a thought from an old hippie:

"If we 'keep it simple' (in our teaching-centered lives), we may find that focusing on substance may make everything easier and bring enduring successes."

From the old hippie,

Robin

18

The Big Rocks

In schools across the country, the holiday season is both a joyous time and a stressful time. At the elementary and middle levels, many students are very excited about the impending holidays and find it difficult to focus. At the same time, these children's teachers are working frantically to cover the entire curriculum that they had planned to teach before the winter break. Like any other school, we have definitely recommitted ourselves to academic achievement as our number one item of core business. Yet we realize that our kids are still kids and that our teachers still have families of their own. Certainly, we make the most of all instructional time allotted to us, but at this time of year, our teachers are more interested in getting through the last two weeks of school as smoothly as possible. It is not a time to consider new teaching strategies. As a result, our last two Friday Focus writings of the year dealt with personal, rather than professional, issues.

The 18th Friday

At our school, much of our core business and professional growth discussions begin with our leadership team, which comprises 10 classroom teachers, four administrators, and one secretary. One of our key teacher leaders on this team is Doris Dickerson, a 7th grade life science teacher and the author of the following Friday Focus.

Rather than share one of her wonderful teaching strategies or the way she plans for authentic formative and summative assessments, Doris chose to write a reflection piece that encouraged us to relax and prioritize our lives. She drew on several authorities on the topic, ranging from Goethe, to John Lennon, to Stephen Covey. All of these disparate authorities know what we know: we always have time for what we put first, so we should place the truly important things in our lives first each day. This holds true both in our personal lives and in our professional lives.

Included in the following writing is a story that another leadership team member and I had shared with the leadership team a week earlier. I was pleased that Doris included it in her own Friday Focus, as this is the point of our leadership team: for teachers to grow as leaders of teachers by taking what we discuss, adding their own ideas, and passing it on to others. Teaching is tough; for our very best teachers, like Doris, it is tougher still, because they work so much harder than our mediocre teachers. While we all need to hear this message, our very best teachers must remember to go with the "big rocks" first and maybe even leave out the smaller ones from time to time.

Friday Focus!

December 10

"Things that matter most should never be at the mercy of things that matter least." Goethe

At this very busy time of year, both personally and professionally, I thought a reflection on the never-ending dimension of time would be very relevant. My message is not one that delves into the Christmas theme, but rather one that has ample application to the holiday season. It happens not only at this time of year, but throughout the year—there just doesn't seem to be enough time to accomplish all that we desire to. Time always has lapsed and continues to lapse for each of us from minute to minute, class period to class period, sunrise to sunset, throughout our lifetime. Do you ever feel stretched for time, like me? Do you leave loose ends at the end of the day? Wonder how you are going to get it all done? I have come to the realization that time constraints will always be present and that I will never get it all done. I know that we all strive to be the best people that we can be. In order to be our best, it is necessary that we take care of ourselves. So what can we do to manage all of our life activities, both professionally and personally? I have come to find comfort in one of Richard Carlson's (1997) many strategies from his book titled, *Don't Sweat the Small Stuff—And It's All Small Stuff.* His strategy (slightly tweaked) is as follows:

Learn to Live in the Present Moment

To a large degree, the measure of our peace of mind is determined by how much we are able to live in the present moment. Irrespective of what happened yesterday or last year and of what may or may not happen tomorrow, the present moment is where you are—always. Without question, many of us have mastered the neurotic art of spending much of our lives worrying about a variety of things all at once. We allow past problems and future concerns to dominate our present moments, so much so that we end up anxious, frustrated, and hopeless. On the flip side, we also postpone our gratification, our stated priorities, and our happiness, often convincing ourselves that someday will be better than today. Unfortunately, the same mental dynamics that tell us to look toward the future will only repeat themselves so that someday will never actually arrive. John Lennon once said, "Life is what's happening when we are busy making other plans." When we are busy making other plans, our children are busy growing up, the people we love are moving away, our bodies are getting out of shape, friends and family members are dying, and our dreams are slipping away. In short, we might miss out on life.

Many people live life as if it were a dress rehearsal for some later date. It isn't. In fact, no one has a guarantee that they will be here tomorrow. Now is the only time we have, and it is the only time over which we have any control. When our attention is in the present moment, we push fear from our minds. Fear is a concern over events that might happen in the future—the copying machine might break, my planning time will be usurped, our students will not meet the standard on the standardized test, and so on.

To combat fear, the best strategy is to learn to bring your attention back to the present. Mark Twain said, "I have been through some terrible times in my life, some of which actually happened." I don't think I can say it any better. Practice keeping your attention on the here and now. Your efforts will pay off in great dividends.

In addition to this strategy, it was very timely (get the pun) that Jeff Zoul and Beth Richardson would share an excerpt from Stephen Covey and colleagues' (Covey, Merrill, & Merrill, 1996) work, *First Things First,* with the leadership team. I would like to share it with you. It is nothing earth-shattering, and perhaps it is nothing that you haven't already heard, but it is worthy to bring once again to the forefront of our minds. The story is called "Put the Big Rocks First."

> At a seminar, the presenter pulled out a wide-mouth gallon jar and placed it next to a pile of fist-sized rocks. After filling the jar to the top with rocks, he asked, "Is the jar full?"
>
> The group replied, "Yes."
>
> He then got some gravel from under the table and added it to the jar. The speaker jiggled the jar until the gravel filled the spaces between the rocks. Again, he asked, "Is the jar full?"
>
> "No!" shouted the group.
>
> Finally, the speaker filled the jar to the brim with water and asked the group the point of this illustration. Someone replied that you could always fit more things into your life if you really worked at it.

"No," countered the speaker. "The point is, if you didn't put the big rocks in first, would you have ever gotten them in?"

As you go through this year, think of the "big rocks" in your life as the things you can do to make this a happier and more productive year for yourself and others. What are your big rocks? Can you identify and define them? List your big rocks, not only for this holiday season, but also for the time to come.

Have a peaceful,
blessed holiday season.

Doris

19

God Bless Us, Every One!

The 19th Friday

This final Friday Focus of the first half of our school year is simply a Holiday card from me to our staff. We had undergone a great deal of change in a short amount of time and responded wonderfully. It is important for school leaders to recognize the accomplishments of the entire staff and to remember not only the professional side of each teacher, but also the personal side.

While I knew I wanted to hit the ground running in the new year and begin sharing even more ideas about teaching and learning, now was a time for something different. Just two weeks before this writing, we lost a teacher on our staff who had fought a long and valiant battle with cancer. Though she had not taught at our school for several months, she was a key member of our family and had touched the lives of every student and teacher with whom she worked. In her will, she even asked that any monetary contributions be dedicated to our school's media center. We subsequently named the media center in her honor. Included in this Friday Focus were remembrances of this beloved teacher by peers who had worked closely with her for years.

Friday Focus!

December 17

"When the dog bites, when the bee stings, when I'm feeling sad, I simply remember my favorite things and then I don't feel so bad."
Rodgers & Hammerstein

It has been said that humans are story-seeking animals. The cultures, religions, and big ideas of ages past have been transmitted from one generation to another through parables, fables, and legends. (Eaker, DuFour, & DuFour, 2002)

The catchy tune "My Favorite Things" from *The Sound of Music* at times garners attention as a Holiday song. At this time of year, it is appropriate indeed that we reflect on all those "favorite things" in our lives. Two of my biggies are OMS students and OMS teachers. Truly, when I am "feeling sad," all I need do is visit any classroom at Otwell and "then I don't feel so bad." Otwell teachers have this same impact on our students, many of whom are happiest during the hours they spend within our building.

You affect students not only by teaching important content, but also by teaching them who you are through your stories, your actions, and your deeds. In speaking with those of you who knew and loved Gwen Gillis, I learned that she was this kind of teacher also, a favorite of kids and colleagues alike. Lisa Lassig shared the following about Gwen:

> "One thing I loved about Gwen was the way she shared stories about herself or her life with the students. We hung on every word!! Would you believe that Gwen scuba dived and came face to face with a shark? Did you know she knew every word to all the rap songs on MTV? Gwen's students loved to hear these stories because it made her a real person whom they could relate to....We left her classroom with a huge smile on our faces and a warm feeling to carry with us the rest of the day."

Our students are truly "story-seeking animals." We have all heard that students want to know how much we care before they care how much we know. Gwen shared this sentiment, as do so many of you. As a result, our students learn a great deal and leave our classrooms with smiling faces on the outside and warm feelings inside.

Jody Boling offers another recollection of working with Gwen:

> "She taught with a love for her subject, a passion for excellent teaching practices, and a sense of humor. She had years of experience, yet sought ideas from others to improve her teaching."

Again, these attributes are in widespread evidence throughout our building today. Master teachers are passionate about their kids as well as their subject matter. Such teachers are always striving to improve professionally, regardless of their current level of expertise. Thank you for engaging in critical dialogue with each other relative to both the art and science of teaching. Thank you for observing in each other's classrooms in an effort to gain new insights into teaching.

I wish you and your families the most joyous of holiday seasons. During the break, I will think of "my favorite things" often and recall the stories you share with your students, your sense of humor, your passion, and your willingness to always improve your practice. Another

OMS friend of Gwen suggested that "Gwen cared...persevered...and found the blessing" each day that she lived. Teachers, thanks for caring. Thanks for persevering through the difficult and stressful times. Thanks for finding blessings even when things appear bleak. It has been a fantastic 2004; I'm looking forward already to seeing you all again for what promises to be an even brighter 2005! We have made a difference with our work here at Otwell *because we* Teach with Passion *each day!*

God bless us, every one!

Jeff

Part 3

The Third Quarter

In a four-quarter basketball game, the two most vitally important times are the first three minutes of the first period and the first three minutes after halftime. It is at these two points that coaches and players establish the direction for the overall game. The school year is not altogether unlike a basketball game in this respect. While every single day is of vital importance and cannot be spent frivolously, the first and third quarters of the school year are perhaps the most important of all. Returning from a one- or two-week winter vacation is a bit like returning to the basketball court after halftime. While we have rested and reflected on how we performed, we have another half ahead of us and much to accomplish in that time. Many opportunities await us, but the challenges have also been clearly identified by now and may well be daunting ones.

The third quarter of this book contains 10 chapters, and more chapters than any other quarter focusing on specific teaching practices such as working with English Speakers of Other Languages (ESOL) students, teaching special education students, differentiating instruction, and improving test scores. Like most school administrators, I stress bell-to-bell instruction and maximizing instruction throughout each of the 180 student school days. However, it seems as if the third quarter of the school year is the most ideal opportunity for accomplishing the greatest amount of teaching and learning, as compared to the other three quarters of the year. The holidays are over, spring break has yet to arrive, our standardized testing dates are still somewhere beyond the horizon, and we have re-energized ourselves over the holiday vacation. It is nuts-and-bolts time for classroom instruction—or as one of my fellow principals likes to call it, a time for focusing on blocking and tackling. It may not be the most glamorous part of the school year—or of our jobs as educators—but it is the most important in terms of providing us an uninterrupted chunk of allotted instructional time.

This is also the point of the year at which I turn over more Friday Focus writings to other leaders at my school. Of the 10 Friday Focus memos in this section of the book, only three are my own, including the first one, which revisits a very important theme: classroom management. For the others, I have called on various staff members who possess specific expertise and insights and are effective at communicating these to their colleagues so that we can best meet the needs of our students—and each other.

20

Managing the Classroom

When I arrived as principal at our school, the overwhelming number one concern among teachers was student discipline. Many teachers insisted that student misbehavior had increased dramatically over the past year or two and that we, as a school, needed to finally address this problem.

Now, I had mixed feelings upon hearing this from teacher after teacher as I met individually with all staff. On the one hand, I knew that the students who attended our school were well above average in every possible area, including test scores and socioeconomic backgrounds. I found it difficult to believe that such students could be behaving so poorly. I also knew that "lack of student discipline" was a common teachers' lament for what was wrong with education at practically every school I visited. At the same time, I knew that this problem was certainly a real one in the estimation of the vast majority of our staff—a staff, by all accounts, respected throughout our school system. I also prided myself during my own teaching and coaching career as one who had a firm grasp on managing the learning environment. I could not tolerate the idea of serving as principal at a school in which teachers felt kids misbehaved and were allowed to get away with irresponsible behavior. I was determined to make student discipline and classroom management a primary point of emphasis for our school throughout my entire first year as principal and beyond.

A Fresh Start

Chances for a fresh start are rare for educators. That is why the first days of the school year are so vitally important in establishing the standards for learning and behavior throughout the year. At our school, we also had a fresh start in the sense that we had a new principal and new assistant principal. This was a chance for me, along with the entire staff, to set the tone for any new expectations we had regarding student behavior and consequences for student misbehavior. Finally, in our school system we had moved up the start of the school year so that we now completed the entire first half of the school year—the first semester—prior to the winter break. As we returned from the holiday vacation, then, we had one final chance for a "mini" fresh start. Although most teachers kept the same students throughout the year, some classes did change. Either way, we had an opportunity to establish fresh expectations for the new semester.

At the beginning of the school year, our teachers were very excited about my emphasis on insisting that students behave and be held accountable for misbehavior. Yet I made it clear that although I would enforce the code of conduct as consistently and firmly as humanly possible, I had much less control over student behavior than each individual teacher did. My main role was to be as visible as possible in every area of our school and to help teachers learn new ways of providing quality instruction and implementing firm, fair, and consistent classroom management techniques. The only tangible change I made in terms of consequences for student misbehavior was to staff an in-school suspension room so that we would have a significant consequence available as an option for serious behavior violations. Everything else we enacted related more to a change in school culture than a change in specific discipline practices.

As we began our second semester together, I felt it important that we revisit the changes in our school culture that had helped to improve student behavior and, as a result, teacher morale.

The 20th Friday

I made it very clear to our three assistant principals that I expected them to enforce code of conduct violations and support teachers when they chose to write office discipline referrals. Of course, I was fortunate that all three of them were already very proficient in this area. Yet I also knew that time spent sitting in the office meting out punishments for student misbehavior was not the best use of these three educators' time. We could improve student behavior much more effectively and efficiently by having the three of them—and me—in the hallways and classrooms of our school instead of in our offices.

In sharing the following survey regarding teacher "discipline" practices, I noticed that only half or so of the 35 items related directly to what we do as teachers to enforce discipline. Instead, most truly do refer to how we manage our classroom environment. If we manage the classroom according to the guidelines suggested, student discipline is for the most part a nonissue. In reading these items, I was struck by how many related to sound teaching and learning practices and how many were touched on as Friday Focus topics: assessment, enthusiasm, motivation, varied learning activities and methods, summarizing learning, giving directions, homework, and an attractive classroom are all points discussed in Friday Focus memos that appear on this survey related to classroom management.

Too often, we hear the words "classroom management" and think about student behavior and issues related to student behavior. In truth, classroom management is just that—managing the classroom, the learning environment. Of course, a well-managed classroom results in little or no student misbehavior. A poorly managed classroom will, on the other hand, encourage student misbehavior.

Friday Focus!

January 7

Teachers have tremendous power to inspire and encourage students, to become strong role models, and to make a decisive difference in students' lives. They also have the power to alienate students. (Spitalli, 2004)

Thoughtful teachers typically have two overall goals. One is to provide a productive climate for student learning and for academic achievement. The second is to foster student satisfaction with schooling. Both are critical aspects of a suitable classroom atmosphere. (Brainard, 2001)

As we begin a new calendar year and a new semester here at school, I wanted to take a moment to revisit the issue of student discipline and classroom management at Otwell Middle School. First off, thank you so much for making this an ongoing point of emphasis throughout the first semester. Through a collective team effort, we have made prodigious strides in improving student behavior and addressing student misbehavior. Obviously, we will never eliminate student behavior indiscretions at the middle school level. However, we must continue to insist that all students adhere to conduct expectations each and every day while at school.

Let's all keep in mind some classroom management basics as we embark upon another semester of schooling. Like most dedicated teachers, I firmly believe that engaging and challenging instruction is the best deterrent to misbehavior. Even our students will tell us that they do not misbehave when the work provided is challenging and interesting. Students also behave better when there is a classroom routine that everyone follows consistently. A well-planned, well-paced lesson will give students little time for disruptive behavior. Plan activities in smaller blocks of time. Set clear limits for your students. Decide what constitutes unacceptable behavior and adhere to these expectations firmly, fairly, and in a friendly manner. Be consistent in enforcing consequences and communicate regularly with parents regarding their child's behavior. Avoid reacting with anger to student misbehavior. Remember Todd Whitaker's (2004) advice to never argue, never yell, and never use sarcasm in dealing with a middle school student.

Remember that student misbehavior generally has some underlying reason. Try to identify and address the cause for the behavior. This lets students know you care for them and gives them a chance to explain and improve their actions. No one—including students themselves—likes classrooms that are characterized by disruptive behavior. Needless to say, such classrooms are also characterized by low-achieving students. At OMS, our students are blessed in that they receive quality instruction on a daily basis in safe and orderly classrooms.

I came across a survey over the holidays that I thought might be an effective way for us to reflect on our individual and collective discipline practices. You might respond with a 1–4 ranking, with 4 indicating "almost always," 3 indicating "frequently," 2 indicating "occasionally," and 1 indicating "almost never." I predict that our teachers will respond with primarily 3s and 4s; thanks again for taking the time to make classroom management an ongoing point of emphasis.

- I am friendly but firm with my students.
- I treat each student with kindness and respect.
- When a student or students act inappropriately, I remain calm and composed.
- I display enthusiasm and a sense of humor with my students.
- During each passing period between classes, I am at the doorway to greet and chat with students.
- I insist that students treat me with dignity and respect.
- I interact with all students, not just a few.
- I give my students a pleasing greeting each day and wish them a pleasant weekend.
- During each passing period between classes, I am at the doorway so I can supervise both the hallway and my classroom.
- So that I know what is going on in my classroom, I generally spend my class time on my feet.

- I expect students to listen attentively when another student or I am talking.
- When I correct student misbehavior, I communicate in a private, positive, and respectful manner.
- I admit that at times student misbehavior is a result of something that was my fault.
- I am able to motivate my students, including the reluctant learner.
- I carefully plan each lesson so that there is no "dead time."
- I provide guided or independent practice during which I move about the room offering individual or small-group assistance.
- During each class period, I provide a variety of learning activities. Rarely do I use an entire period for a single activity, as students need a change of pace.
- I adjust my daily lesson planning to take into account my students' span of attention.
- I think through discipline decisions before acting.
- I make only those discipline decisions that I can enforce.
- I make discipline decisions after the "heat of the moment" has passed.
- When a student misbehaves in class, I find a way to correct the behavior privately, perhaps by moving near the student and whispering a correction.
- While I take attendance or perform other necessary tasks, often at the outset of each class session, my students are working independently, perhaps on a brief assignment or problem on the overhead or board.
- I establish time-saving routines for collecting papers and distributing materials or supplies.
- My directions for a learning activity are brief and concise.
- I give directions one step at a time. I avoid long and detailed directions.
- I show sincere enthusiasm for the subjects I teach.
- I provide a neat classroom that gives students the idea of orderliness.
- I present a professional appearance in the classroom.
- I insist that my students maintain high standards in their work and behavior. In both areas, my standards are realistic and attainable.

- Because there is no "best" teaching method, my methods and learning activities are many and varied.
- My homework assignments have a purpose, are instructional, and are regulated as to the time it will take a student to complete the assignment.
- I make my classroom attractive by having effective bulletin boards related to the topics being studied at the particular time.
- During each class session, I summarize, or have students summarize, the day's learning.
- I use pretests or other procedures to ascertain what students already know.

Thank you for taking the time to informally self-assess your practices that affect student behavior; I hope this exercise reminds us of how best to manage the learning environment so that student misbehavior is kept to a minimum. Please let me know of any ideas you have in this area throughout the year. *Teach with Passion* each day this semester!

Have an awesome weekend!

Jeff

21

Strategies for ESOL Students

No school that I know of serves students from only one ethnic background or one socioeconomic subgroup. Our own school is much more homogeneous than most, with 85 percent of our student population identified as Caucasian. Yet it is striking to note that only a decade earlier, this same figure was nearly 100 percent. In our school community, we are experiencing rapid growth in our Spanish-speaking population. Among this student subgroup, a significant number arrive classified as Limited English Proficient (LEP) and are served through our English Speakers of Other Languages (ESOL) program.

With the onset of the federal No Child Left Behind (NCLB) act, educators have undergone a paradigm shift whereby we now must meet the needs of all learners and prove that we are reaching specific academic achievement standards in the areas of math, reading, and English language arts. While many educators across the country bemoan the stringent requirements associated with NCLB, at our school, we embrace these as a way in which we can prove that "The Otwell Way" is more than a trite saying; rather, it is the way we go about welcoming every student, regardless of background or ability level, and do whatever it takes to see that he or she succeeds.

The 21st Friday

We are fortunate to have two certified ESOL teachers serving our students expertly and educating the rest of the staff in how best to work with our LEP population. Our ESOL teachers work with students both in an inclusion setting and in a pull-out resource model, depending on the needs of individual students. One of our ESOL teachers, Mary Ann Douglas, authored the following Friday Focus. She began with a quote similar to one shared in Chapter 13 by another teacher leader in introducing the CRISS strategies for learning about learning. Mary Ann also mentions CRISS. In perusing the strategies she offered, one realizes the obvious application benefits they have for any teacher working with ESOL students. However, much of what she shared also makes sense for those of us working with any student who is trying to learn a difficult concept.

Our teachers took particular interest in Mary Ann's recommendation that we remember the "Five Rs" when working with our LEP students. Certainly, repeating, rephrasing, reiterating, restating, and rewording are valuable teaching points to keep in mind when working with students who are limited in their English skills. At the same time, we realize that these are cornerstones of effective teaching practices when working with any student.

The "bag of tricks" to use when teaching ESOL students that Mary Ann shared with teachers are practical and helpful. She also reinforced a value of our faculty when she thanked teachers for both helping our ESOL students learn English as well as for maintaining "The Otwell Way." Part of that "way" is making sure we connect with all students by helping them connect what they learn with their own lives.

Friday Focus!

January 14

"Tell me, and I forget. Show me, and I may remember. Involve me, and I will understand." Chinese proverb

All people smile in the same language. (Adams & Johnson, 1997)

Have you ever asked yourself, "What am I supposed to do with this person if he or she can't even understand what I'm saying?" Well, I've been in your shoes, too. I'm a mother *and* a wife! Your applause is sincerely appreciated!

Seriously, we can and must find a way to reach ESOL students. One way we can do so is by considering the following specific recommendations for ESOL student instruction as outlined in the *Georgia ESOL Resource Guide* (Georgia Department of Education, 2005).

- First, remember the Five Rs:
  Repeat, Rephrase, Reiterate, Restate, Reword!!
- Choose a proficient American student (of the same gender) to serve as the ESOL student's partner.
- Provide cloze technique passages (some words missing) for the LEP student to complete from the regular text or lecture notes.
- Have the ESOL student view videos or filmstrips or listen to CDs or cassettes of the content.
- Use brain-based learning (invoking multiple intelligences) with lessons that include hands-on activities, choral reading, songs,

chants, dance, drawing, mapmaking, labeling, or graphic organizers; these are all staples of a rich language-learning environment.

- Use hand signals to accompany verbal instructions and augment any materials with pantomime and gestures. Perhaps you can work out a secret signal the ESOL student can use when he or she doesn't understand.

- Remember schematic sets for acquisition of new vocabulary. Avoid introducing new words out of context. Visual representations are also recommended whenever possible.

- Use power writing and CRISS strategies in the content areas. Use fewer pronouns. Repetition of key concepts is essential. The use of the imperative or command form of verbs is easier to understand. Avoid use of conditionals—these may cause confusion.

We also realize that some of our ESOL students are currently unable to be assessed in the same manner in which we assess our native English speakers. *The Classroom Teacher's ESL Survival Packet* (Kentucky Migrant Technology Project, 1997) offers specific assessment modification tips, which we can and should use in order to help our students and ourselves. Chief among these practices is the idea that we should assess ESOL students according to what they can do, rather than what they cannot do.

Technique: Modifications

- Test key concepts or main ideas.
- Avoid test questions asking for discrete information.
- Make a simplified language version of the test.
- Simplify instructions.
- Provide word banks.
- Give students extra time to complete tests.
- Give students objective tests: matching, multiple choice, etc.
- Make all or part of the test a demonstration or oral response.

Technique: Alternate Assessment Strategies for ESOL Students

1. Nonverbal
   - Physical demonstration (point, gesture, act out, thumbs up or down, nod yes or no)
   - Pictorial products (manipulate or create drawings, draw diagrams, make dioramas, design pamphlets, build models, draw graphs, make charts, label pictures, keep a picture journal, write an alphabet book, create an acrostic, etc.)

- KWL charts using pictures or native language
2. Oral and Written Strategies
   - Interviews, oral reports, or role plays using visual cues, gestures, or physical activity
   - Describing, explaining, summarizing, retelling, paraphrasing
   - Thinking and learning logs
   - Reading response logs
   - Writing assignments
   - Dialogue journals
   - Audio or video recordings of students
   - Portfolios

I can assure you that drawing on this bag of tricks will likely help you make a connection that will, in turn, make a difference in the academic progress and development of your ESOL students. Perhaps you may even be instrumental in their desire to persist and be successful in their new culture. Thank you all for being here to give our ESOL students the opportunity to learn a new language and to become part of "The Otwell Way."

Happy Weekend!

Mary Ann

22

Working with
Special Needs Students

In the Friday Focus writings we send out each week, at times I try to group together two or more weeks anchored by a common theme. Like the previous week's Friday Focus, this week's addressed the needs of another at-risk population at our school: special needs students. Chapter 21's Friday Focus was written by one of our ESOL experts; this week's was penned by our special education department chairperson. As noted earlier with regard to ESOL students, every school is changing to meet the needs of a widely diverse student population. At our school, just over 10 percent of the student population is classified as "special education." We have students identified with specific learning disabilities and behavior disorders along with students labeled "mildly mentally handicapped" and "severely and profoundly mentally handicapped." It is our mission and our passion that they all learn to the very best of their capabilities.

The 22nd Friday

The following Friday Focus was written by Pam Poe, who has taught special education for years at our school. She is also the department chair for special education and is widely respected in our school and community as an outstanding teacher and an even more incredible human being. Much as Mary Ann did in the Friday Focus dealing with ESOL strategies in Chapter 21, Pam offered many specific ideas for teachers to consider when working with special education students. Once again, any good teacher will recognize that these strategies apply to some extent to all learners, not only special education students.

The primary focus of Pam's writing was twofold. First, she equated working with students to playing the game of baseball. How can baseball apply to the classroom? For one thing, both can be exciting places to visit with fun activities going on. For another, the concept of teamwork is essential to both. One can compare the school year to a nine-inning game, breaking it down into smaller segments of learning. I have even observed some teachers using a "three strikes" system effectively to monitor student behavior. Finally, we have one teacher at our school who takes baseball's traditional seventh-inning stretch and incorporates it into her classroom. Several times throughout her 90-minute block, she has students stand and take a "seven-second stretch" to refocus students on the learning task at hand. I, myself, always refer to the first day of school as "Opening Day." Nearly all students enjoy, or are at least very familiar with, the game of baseball and other sports. There are endless ways to incorporate sports analogies and strategies into our classrooms.

In addition, and perhaps more importantly, Pam stressed the simple concept of caring and described specifically what we can do to show our students that we care. As anyone who reads this book knows, we have a caring staff at our school, and we tend to go above and beyond the call of duty in giving to our students and our community. Of course, like all schools, we have some teachers who are not as passionate about what they do as we would prefer. Pam's suggestions below served as a reminder to our very best teachers and as motivation to others to act in accordance with the values shared by the vast majority of our "team."

According to Pam, one way we can take caring to the next level is by enlisting the help of our colleagues. She went on to mention several by name who have special skills and who contribute in some special way to help students in need. At our school, we work hard to cultivate a collaborative approach to learning, whereby we can rely on each other as needed. Just as in baseball, we all need a pinch hitter or a relief pitcher periodically, and it may well be when we are working with our most challenging special needs students.

Friday Focus!

January 21

"Seek first to understand, then to be understood." Stephen Covey

"To affect the quality of the day, that is the highest of arts."
Henry David Thoreau

Students with learning problems need constant motivation in order to learn. For the teacher, this task can seem nearly impossible and exhausting, especially when students enter your classroom with *no* materials but *lots* of baggage—past failures, academic frustrations, and less-than-ideal attitudes.

Robert Harris (1991), a writer and educator with more than 25 years of teaching experience, writes about how what we do in our classrooms can be compared to the game of baseball:

Think about a group of young people playing a baseball game. The very things that motivate them to work hard and do well playing baseball can be adapted to the classroom:

- *Teamwork:* Young people like working as a team. Yet often the learning activities we assign call for individual effort. By designing more team assignments, we can reap the benefits of teamwork. The weaker students will learn by having others help them. And, since teaching someone something is the best way to learn, the students who teach each other will learn better than if they were learning alone.

- *Fun:* Sports are fun, exciting, and highly emotional. Learning experiences should be, too. Strong and lasting memory is connected with the emotional state and experience of the learner. People remember more when the learning is accompanied by strong emotions.

- *Enjoyment of Success:* Playing a game provides a constant flow of accomplishments. Even the players on the losing team enjoy a strikeout, a good hit, a great catch. Breaking learning into smaller parts that can more easily be conquered, producing feelings of accomplishment and success, will help motivate students to go forward, even through very difficult material.

- *Activity:* A baseball game is definitely not passive—it requires both mental and physical activity. Teachers should strive to make learning always mentally active and often physically active as well.

- *Flexibility and Creativity:* Baseball has rules, but within those rules the players have a range of choices and strategies for accomplishing a given goal. Students learn better when the directions have some flexibility and they can put some of "themselves" into the assignment.

On a more personal level, I have tried countless strategies to motivate low-performing students with varying degrees of success and high levels of frustration (mostly mine). The one strategy that consistently works for me, though, is *caring*. I do know that we are all caring individuals, or else we wouldn't be in this noble profession called teaching. What I'm talking about, though, is taking caring to the next level:

- *Allowing ourselves to be human in front of our students.* Share stories, lessons learned, mistakes made. Young people are quite insecure at this age—they need to see the person, not just the teacher or authority figure.

- *Developing a relationship with our students.* Try to learn about your students' lives outside of school. It can make a world of difference, especially when their home situation is less than ideal.
- *Setting goals with individual students.* For one student, it might be an attendance goal. For another, it might concern disruptive behavior. And remember to check on their progress—your concern and approval might be the only reward needed.
- Enlisting the help of your colleagues.

It truly "takes a village" for special needs children, because they require that constant push. There are so many examples right here at Otwell. I have seen Phil Westray mentor some mighty challenging boys over the years, with great success. I see Kathy Ciavarelli smoothly lead a three-ring circus each morning as she helps students get their makeup work completed. I know that my lowest students beg to take Mr. Z.'s technology class and Niyelo because they are successful in these classes. I know that Allison Rauscher can pull some quality work out of the toughest eighth grade boys, and that she loves every minute of it. I know that our coaches support academics and make sure the players know their expectations. I know that Tom Pelky works to match struggling kids with eighth grade peer buddies, and that it is helping. I count myself blessed to be among each of you and learn from you daily.

Just don't give up, for long after the content has been forgotten, the teacher will be remembered.

Pam

23

More Classroom Management

It may seem as if we spent a great deal of time on classroom management issues in our Friday Focus writings throughout the year. Well, first of all, this is true. Although we have great kids and an awesome teaching staff, we are always searching for better ways to rein in our kids' predilection for unbridled—and sometimes over the top—enthusiasm, both for learning and for inappropriate behaviors. In addition, as I noted earlier, the issue of student behavior had been a huge concern for the entire staff during the preceding school year. By all accounts, we had made great strides in this area during our first semester together, and I definitely wanted to begin the second semester reiterating what makes us successful in the area of classroom management.

The Paradox of Time

Interestingly, teachers at every school who offer the least in terms of positive contributions are the very same teachers who complain that "there simply isn't enough time" for anything else. Meanwhile, our very finest teachers always seem to make time to go the extra mile on behalf of a student, a colleague, or the school as a whole. I am reminded of a friend's comment to me recently. He is in another line of work, and he needed an important new project to be completed almost immediately. He called on his busiest employee to tackle this additional project, stating, "If you want something done, call on a busy person." Unfortunately, at every school with which I have been associated, some teachers simply work harder than others. For professionals working in a field in which everyone earns income according to the same salary schedule, this does not always seem fair, yet it has been and will likely remain the reality of education.

While our most effective teachers may not always reap the financial rewards they deserve, they gain much more significant, though intangible, benefits. Their students, colleagues, and parents show them much more respect and affection. Their students learn more and are better behaved. The very same students who create daily disturbances in one teacher's classroom can move across the hall at the sound of a bell and begin behaving flawlessly for another. When we see this happening, we know it is not an accident or due to good fortune. Instead, it is the result of hard work, including careful planning, staying current with best practices, and constantly reflecting on what is and is not working well. Classroom management is definitely one component of teaching that requires careful planning and reflection.

This was the last time during the school year in which I directly wrote about classroom management issues in the Friday Focus. I wanted to follow up on the first Friday Focus of the semester (see Chapter 20), which also related to classroom management and included a survey for teachers regarding their practices in this area. While many teachers take time to really absorb our weekly memos, I know that others likely skim them only briefly. This issue was much too important to our school community to overlook, and I wanted to make sure that the entire staff understood that.

Ironically, the teachers who take the time to carefully pore over and reflect on each week's writing are those teachers who are already working harder and longer than other teachers who cannot find the time to read each Friday Focus deeply. Many others have observed what I have noticed about those with whom we work: teachers who merely do the bare minimum rarely have time to take on any additional responsibilities. They are simply "too busy" (yet they manage to find time for complaining). On the other hand, our exemplary teachers somehow always find time to take on yet another task or responsibility as long as they feel it will help a student, our school, or their own performance as a teacher (not surprisingly, these teachers *are* too busy for one thing: complaining).

Interestingly, classroom management is an example of the phenomenon described above. Our very best teachers, of course, are already quite proficient in the area of classroom management. Yet they are the ones who are most appreciative when I send out a Friday Focus on the topic. They wish to become even better at maintaining an optimal learning environment for their students—and themselves. The few teachers at our school who are deficient in this area are the ones who would likely not take the time to read the following suggestions very carefully or adjust their practices in any way. One goal of several Friday Focus writings devoted to the topic of classroom management and student discipline was to get all teachers talking about—and focusing on—this all-important issue. Even our least diligent teachers want their kids to behave; our very best teachers insist on it and expect our entire school to consistently adhere to best practices in this area.

The 23rd Friday

In this week's Friday Focus, I began with a quotation that suggests just how important classroom management is in terms of its influence on student learning. We have many exciting and new initiatives that we have implemented within our school system. Assessment for learning (AFL), high leverage strategies (HLS), professional appraisal cycle (PAC), professional learning communities (PLC), and interactive whiteboards are but a few of the new theories, practices, and technological advances that we have studied or adopted and that are familiar to any teacher employed in our school system. These all help us to become better at what we do, and our teachers have worked hard learning about these new ideas and putting them into practice. At the same time, without a well-managed classroom, none of the above means a whole lot in terms of student learning or teacher performance.

The following writing focused on four simple characteristics of a well-managed classroom with which nearly any educator would agree. The key, of course, is getting every teacher at our schools to adhere to them. I mentioned that students generally know right from wrong and that they want us to deal with their peers who misbehave. Our teachers, too, know right from wrong. Our best ones also expect us to deal with those few who do not adhere to shared values in this key area. At our school, teachers had identified improved student behavior as a goal and we were relentless in seeing to it that we all worked together to achieve this goal.

Friday Focus!

January 28

In a study reviewing 11,000 pieces of research that spanned 50 years, three researchers determined that there are 28 factors which influence student learning and these have been rank ordered. The most important factor governing student learning is classroom management. (Wang, Haertel, & Walberg, 1993/1994)

Wow! As with most research we see, who knows what is really true? Yet I tend to agree with the above statement. Sure, we all realize the importance of AFL, HLS, PLC, PAC, multiple intelligences, differentiated instruction, and even interactive whiteboards. And, sure, all of the above can be related to classroom management. Still, if a classroom is not well managed in the traditional sense of an orderly learning environment, optimal student learning simply will not occur.

Classroom management is something that has always been a passion of mine. Like many of you, as a teacher I designed creative lessons with many opportunities for engaging (and even fun) quality student work and activities. But we cannot accomplish this until we have set forth clear expectations for student behavior and performance. So many of you are masters at both that I am humbled to work in your presence. Last semester, we spent a great deal of time and energy talking about student discipline and insisting that all students conform to firm, fair, and consistent expectations. While we have not spent as much time recently discussing this vitally important topic, please do not neglect classroom management as one of our foremost responsibilities. We are entering a phase of the school year when many of our children are becoming comfortable with the new year. For some of our students, this is swell; for others, that comfort level may mean they are ready to misbehave. Teachers, please do not allow this to occur. Address such situations immediately. In addition, when students chronically misbehave or commit a single negative act of a serious nature, they should be referred to Beth, Suzanne, Van, or me for consequences. As we go forth throughout this year, hold firm to our expectations that all students will exhibit proper behavior.

Characteristics of a Well-Managed Classroom

In a well-managed classroom, the following can be observed:

- Students are deeply involved with their work, especially with academic, teacher-led instruction.
- Students know what is expected of them and are generally successful.
- There is relatively little wasted time, confusion, or disruption.
- The climate of the classroom is work-oriented, but relaxed and pleasant.

Does this sound like the typical OMS classroom? As one who walks in every classroom every week, I can honestly answer in the affirmative. Let's work together to keep this a reality.

Additional thoughts on classroom management that I find worth revisiting are tidbits of advice I gleaned from Todd Whitaker's work (2004). In a nutshell, the best teachers focus on expectations. Other teachers focus on rules. The least effective teachers focus on consequences (remember, this does *not* mean students should not be written up and punished for behavior indiscretions when appropriate, but the *focus* is on our expectations). Effective teachers establish clear expectations at the start of the year and consistently follow them throughout the year. The key is to set expectations and then establish relationships so that students want to meet these expectations. Great teachers do not focus on what they will do when kids misbehave. Instead, they expect good behavior, and that is generally what they get.

For the most part, our students know the difference between right and wrong and want teachers to deal with their peers who misbehave. Of course, at this age, they also want their peers treated with dignity and respect, but they will always be on the side of the teacher who firmly, fairly, and consistently adheres to high expectations for student comportment. Already this semester, I have met with over 30 students sent to the office on positive discipline referrals. This is an awesome way to start the new year off right—by recognizing students who are behaving well and serving as role models for their peers. It will also serve you well should you need to reprimand these same students at a later date for a behavior faux pas. While the positive discipline referral program has served us well, we are also realists and know that Beth, Suzanne, and Van will receive referrals of another variety as the year progresses. Treat students with dignity and respect no matter how they behave. At the same time, insist that they, too, treat us and their peers with dignity and respect and hold them accountable to this standard. Another reason I love working at Otwell is because our teachers are masters at maintaining exemplary classroom management practices. Establishing a safe, orderly, and well managed classroom allows us to *Teach with Passion* each day!

Happy Weekend!

Jeff

24

Responding to Learners

The 24th Friday

In an earlier Friday Focus (see Chapter 21), one of our ESOL teachers shared several strategies for working with our LEP population. She encouraged us to keep in mind what she termed the "Five Rs": repeat, rephrase, reiterate, restate, and reword. As I mentioned in that chapter, these reminders are helpful in working with all learners, not just our ESOL students. In this week's Friday Focus, Ezel Harrell, an eighth grade math teacher and our math department chairperson, once again focused on the letter "R" by sharing what she had learned at another school where she worked. The "Three Rs" shared below are not unlike the Five Rs shared earlier. Ezel called on teachers to use language that reinforces, reminds, and redirects students.

In her Friday Focus writing, Ezel shared specific situations that occur in both the hallways of a school and in classrooms to show how teachers might respond effectively to students. While even she admitted to periodically falling into the trap of simply demanding that students behave a certain way or accomplish a certain task, she reminded us that students are likely to respond more positively if we respond to them more appropriately.

While earlier Friday Focus writings discussed in a general way how we manage the learning environment, Ezel shared a way in which she puts solid theory into practical everyday use within her own classroom. Finally, in keeping with her theme of the letter "R," she cleverly closed her Friday Focus by encouraging teachers to have a "three-R" weekend.

Friday Focus!

February 4

"Each of us is called to make the world a better place. To do so, our lives must be creative." Father Edward J. Lavin, Jesuit priest

How do we manage our students' learning and behavior on a continuous basis? Each day, I find myself questioning how I am relating to our students, both on an academic level and on a personal level. How can I improve the exchange that takes place between us? How can I pose questions to make students want to think for themselves? How can I show students how to communicate their needs effectively? How will that impact the exchanges they have with their peers, with people in the community, and with family and friends? Consider the exchange between a principal and students below:

Heading up the stairway, the principal notices two children heading down. They are happily slip-sliding and jumping steps. They are so involved in their "sport," they don't notice the adult until she demands that they stop. Just as she is about to launch into lecture mode, she decides to try out the Responsive Classroom approach to language (Horsch, Chen, & Wagner, 2002) she is learning in workshops.

"Remind me," she asks one of the boys, "how do we go down the stairs in our school in a safe way?"

"One step at a time?" he says.

"Okay. Show me how it looks when you do that," she tells the other boy. He walks back up the stairs and comes down with precise steps.

"Exactly," she says. "And why is that important?"

"So we are safe."

"So we keep others safe."

She nods her agreement. "Think you can do that now and keep yourselves and everyone else safe?"

They nod in solemn assent and set off, one step at a time. Seeing them in such good control, she thinks to herself, "I like this. It works."

What the principal above is referring to is using language to encourage and empower students. How often do we merely direct students to perform a task or complete an assignment? So much of what our kids learn from us is modeled behavior. The importance of students learning how to express themselves using language is monumental and is oftentimes much longer-lasting than the specific curriculum objectives we teach.

There are three basic tenets according to the Responsive Classroom philosophy (Horsch, Chen, & Wagner, 2002) for showing our students how to use language that will empower them and provide encouragement. These are called the Three Rs: reinforcing, reminding, and redirecting. I hear many of us using language that accomplishes this, providing our students a strong foundation for making good choices in school and beyond on a daily basis. Some of the general characteristics of encouraging and empowering language include the following:

- Be specific and direct. ("We will start when I see everyone's eyes on Jason.")

- Speak to the students rather than about the students. ("Leila, I noticed you stayed in your seat while I talked to Derek. Thanks for your cooperation.")

- Stress the deed, not the doer. Describe actions and deeds rather than making judgments. ("I notice a lot of paper on the floor. We can't leave the room until it is clean.")

- Give students the opportunity to follow through with appropriate behavior. ("Show me how you can do that appropriately.")

- Frame a positive action and choice. ("You can walk slowly and quietly with your friends, or you can walk next to me.")

In a perfect world, we would use constructive language (and methods like the Three Rs) during every exchange with our students, yet I still find myself sometimes reduced to "Just do it because I told you to!" Reality dictates that we do the best we can in each and every situation we encounter. We have the most dedicated, professional, student-oriented staff imaginable at OMS—you all do a fabulous job managing the interactions you have with your students. Keep doing what it is you do best—exhibiting passion for our kids and their learning!

Have a relaxing, restful,
and rejuvenating weekend!

Ezel

25

Striving for Great

As a middle school and high school English teacher, one of my goals was to serve as a model for my students through my own reading. I was always reading what I considered to be serious literature and would often discuss with my students what I was reading, even passing on to them books I had read that I thought they, too, might enjoy. As a school administrator, I still try to read a great deal and still find myself sharing whatever I read that is useful with others. Now, however, instead of sharing primarily with students, I more often find myself sharing what I read and what I learn about our profession through my reading with teachers.

Leading or Managing?

Immediately after assuming the role of principal at our school, I changed the focus of our school's leadership team just slightly. It seemed as if we were spending too much time on managerial issues and not enough time on instructional concerns. As a result, I kept the biweekly, 90-minute schedule for leadership team meetings that was already in place, but changed our team's priorities by reserving the first 60 minutes of each meeting for discussion about a big-picture, yearlong instructional focus and the remaining 30 minutes on operational issues that were also urgent, but not as important as our instructional goals.

The leadership team had embarked on a yearlong study of the book *Professional Learning Communities at Work* by DuFour and Eaker (1998). At this point in the school year, much of what we had studied and learned from this book through our leadership team meetings had filtered down to the rest of our staff. We were already looking ahead to the next school year, when we would implement the professional learning communities concept as a schoolwide initiative. In the meantime, we continued to study learning communities and share what we learned with others.

Another book that had influenced me greatly at this time and that I wanted to share with our teachers was *Good to Great* by Jim Collins (2001). Although the book is intended for the corporate community, I had found much of Collins's advice applicable to schools. Perhaps the most valuable insight I received from this book is the affirmation that if we had effective people at our school, such people would not need to be tightly managed. Instead, we needed only to provide a certain vision for what we wanted to achieve and allow our teachers the freedom to succeed.

The 25th Friday

Although nearly all of our teachers had studied the writings of noted educational leaders referred to throughout the year's Friday Focus writings, few were familiar with the work of Jim Collins. It was stunning to me how closely his work paralleled what we had been trying to accomplish at our school. Many of his themes mirrored those we had been emphasizing in our meetings, in our discussions, and in our weekly writings. In the following writing, I focused on one small but powerful aspect of Collins's book, the three themes of discipline within an organization: disciplined people, disciplined thought, and disciplined action. We certainly had a school staffed with an overwhelming percentage of disciplined people. Our goal was to channel our efforts in a collective manner by thinking deeply about the issues that faced our school and then—after gaining consensus—putting these thoughts and ideas into action.

Friday Focus!

February 11

If you have the right people on the bus, the problem of how to motivate and manage people largely goes away. The right people do not need to be tightly managed or fired up; they will be self-motivated by the inner drive to produce the best results and to be part of creating something great. (Collins, 2001)

From 1982 to 2001, I read over 100 novels each year. Reading has always been one of my foremost passions, never more so than when I was teaching high school and middle school English. In 2002, however, I began reading many books on leadership and education in addition to reading novels. With my EdS studies followed by my doctoral studies and their concomitant reading requirements, I suddenly realized that something had to go. In perusing one of John Maxwell's many great texts on leadership (1998), I noted with dismay his own struggles with time management. He, too, realized that some things simply had to be removed from his plate, and he reluctantly ceased reading fiction of any type as one way to free up some time. Upon reading this confession, I immediately did likewise, and for two years now, I have not completed a novel. I still manage to read my 100 books per year, but during this time, nearly all have been books on leadership or education. If I ever finally complete my doctoral degree, I will immediately begin reading fiction—and fiction only—for several years.

Of all the books on education and leadership I devoured in this time period, one that still stands out as powerfully important is Jim Collins's (2001) *Good to Great.* Ironically, this is a book written for business leaders, not teachers. Collins analyzed companies that go from good to great, studying 1,435 companies that appeared in the *Fortune* 500 from 1965 to 1995. Of these 1,435 companies, Collins and his research team found only 11 that had enjoyed sustained financial success for a minimum of 15 years. Collins's research is essentially a story of passion, focus, inquiry, and action—collectively pursued. Many of his findings are also applicable to schools and school leaders (which includes all 100 Otwell Middle School employees, as we all play a leadership role of some sort). In a nutshell, Collins identifies six core factors of success that he organizes into the three themes of disciplined people, disciplined thought, and disciplined action. The visual below represents his conceptual framework:

Level 5 Leadership	First Who, Then What	Confront the Brutal Facts	The Hedgehog Concept	Culture of Discipline	Technology Accelerates
Disciplined People		Disciplined Thought		Disciplined Action	

At Otwell, I think we all take pride in being disciplined professionals committed to our craft. Through our work this year with professional learning communities, my hope is that we will take advantage of this given and further enhance our opportunities for disciplined thought and disciplined action. Two characteristics that OMS teachers exhibit, which Collins refers to as the foundations of "Level 5 leadership," are professional will and personal humility. Two examples of how we display these sides of discipline follow:

Professional Will

- Demonstrating an unwavering resolve to do whatever must be done to produce the best long-term results, no matter how difficult.
- Looking in the mirror, not out the window, to apportion responsibility for poor results—never blaming other people, external factors, or bad luck.

Personal Humility

- Acting with quiet, calm determination. Relying principally on inspired standards to motivate us.
- Looking out the window, not in the mirror, to apportion credit for the success of the organization—to other people, external factors, and good luck.

In emphasizing that a culture of discipline is paramount to corporate success, Collins notes that successful organizations continually use words like *disciplined, rigorous, dogged, determined, diligent, precise, fastidious, systematic, methodical, workmanlike, demanding, consistent, focused, accountable,* and *responsible* (do these sound like words that apply to OMS teachers, by any chance?). The single most important form of discipline for sustained results is fanatical adherence to three intersecting circles Collins terms "The Hedgehog Concept." Within these three intersecting circles are the following questions:

- What are we deeply passionate about?
- What do we do best?
- What drives our engine?

Successful organizations focus only on these three ideas and are willing to shun opportunities that do not fall within these three circles. Please allow me to share three final thoughts from *Good to Great* on sustaining a culture of organizational discipline:

- A culture of discipline involves a duality. It requires people who adhere to a constrained system, yet it gives people freedom and responsibility within the framework of that system.
- A culture of discipline is not just about action. It is about getting disciplined *people* who engage in disciplined *thought* and who then take disciplined *action.*
- The *Good to Great* companies appear boring and pedestrian-looking from the outside, but upon closer inspection, they are full of people who display extreme diligence and a stunning intensity.

It is indeed tempting to view ourselves already as a great school. In many ways we certainly are. Yet I prefer the idea that we are a good school moving toward greatness and that the wonderful work we do during the remainder of this year will push us closer to that goal. Remembering what we are passionate about, what we are best at, and what drives our engine are three ways we establish professional discipline and three ways we *Teach with Passion* each day!

Happy Weekend!

Jeff

26

ESOL Revisited

One of the greatest challenges we face at our school is keeping up with the best way to serve our rapidly increasing ESOL population. While educators at some schools may be apprehensive or even resentful about working with students who do not speak English well, at our school we take pride in welcoming such students and leading the way for other schools in our system in getting these students to meet or exceed academic standards.

Prior to arriving at Otwell Middle School, I had very limited experience in working with ESOL students. I have learned a great deal since then, both from our ESOL teachers and from our ESOL students themselves. The most important thing I have learned is that the vast majority of our ESOL students are much like the vast majority of our other students. They are respectful and hardworking, and they want to learn. While our teachers are masterful at somehow managing to reach ESOL students of all levels, teaching students who simply do not yet understand the English language continues to be a difficult and, at times, frustrating challenge for us. One thing we try to remember during those frustrating times is that we can and should rely on each other for support.

The 26thFriday

Brent Agnew authored the following Friday Focus, which may be one of my very favorite editions. One reason I so enjoy Brent's writing is that he managed to capture both the art and the science behind teaching discussed in Chapter 14. In this case, he specifically addressed both the art and science of teaching our students who have yet to acquire academic English skills. I also liked the gentle, yet effective, way in which Brent acknowledged those teachers who may "roll their eyes" while reading his perspective on the long and arduous process of learning a language. My own father spoke only Czech until he began public school as a 6-year–old, and to this day he thinks that such students should—like him—simply be expected to magically acquire our language. However, while I certainly respect my father's perspective on the subject, Brent relied on sound research and years of personal experience in making a compelling case against such thinking. In Chapter 21, Mary Ann

Douglas set the stage for helping teachers who work with ESOL students. Here, Brent took us a step further, sharing research findings, strategies, comparisons, and personal experiences.

One idea that Brent shared which is a powerful reminder for all teachers is the "i + 1" philosophy of teaching language. As we have said several times throughout this book, what works for one segment of the student population often works for all segments of the student population. What Brent shared in terms of this new idea is yet another example. Brent closed his writing with descriptions of ESOL students at our school. While these descriptions were compilations, rather than actual individual students, they were all based on students who were enrolled at our school at the time of this writing. The final student description is of an ESOL student who had been referred for Horizons, the gifted program at our school. Having students who qualify for ESOL services as well as gifted services has been both a triumph and an eye-opener for teachers at our school. Much of our success in working with ESOL learners can be attributed to the level of awareness our staff has, thanks to Brent and several other teachers on staff who are certified experts in this area and who share their expertise freely and regularly.

Friday Focus!

February 18

[Academic language is] the phonology, vocabulary, grammar, semantics, pragmatics, and discourse (formal thought patterns) of English across all four language skills—listening, speaking, reading, and writing—increasing in cognitive complexity across each subject area with each succeeding grade level. Developing proficiency in academic language thus means catching up and keeping up with native speakers for eventual successful academic performance at secondary and university levels of instruction—a monumental achievement. (Collier, 1995)

I feel that this quote from Virginia Collier (1995) a decade ago still helps explain how it can take between 7 and 10 years to acquire academic English. As ESOL teachers, Mary Ann and I are required by the state to present an annual presentation to teachers for professional development. Each year, our presentation includes the fact that it takes a minimum of years to acquire the language needed to succeed in school. Each year, I wonder how many teachers may be rolling their eyes at this piece of data. It seems a little long, don't ya think?!? It certainly seems that a student learns enough language to understand what is going on around him or her within a couple of years if that student really wants to. I understand. Then I remember that I've been working on my Spanish for 13 years and would fail horribly at a university-level class in Mexico in any content area.

A couple of terms, basic interpersonal communicative skills (BISC) and cognitive academic language proficiency (CALP), have floated around the field of teaching English to speakers of other languages. These were coined by Jim Cummins (1984) more than 25 years ago, but he has elaborated on them with a diagram developed to expand on the terminology:

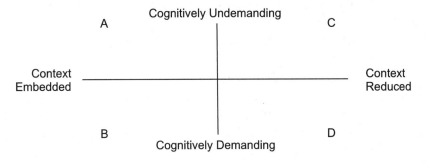

In a context-embedded setting, such as following a schedule, participants can negotiate meaning. In a context-reduced setting, such as reading a textbook or completing a worksheet, participants cannot negotiate meaning. Cognitively demanding and undemanding are self-explanatory.

Mastering Quadrant A may take six months to a year itself for many students. Quadrant B and C can take up to two to five years, depending on the student. Quadrant D, the academic language, takes up to 10 years.

I hear you responding, "Okay Brent, that's great, but how does this pessimistic bit of reality help me help the ESOL students in the classroom?" Well, in the back of my mind, I have always kept the idea of "i + 1." This is a concept that states that if you want to teach a language to a student, you speak at this level, where "i" is what they already know and "+ 1" is going just beyond it. It's a lot easier for me in my small classes, where I get to know the students and their capacity for learning on a very personal level. It's a lot more difficult in your classes, where the ESOL students may make up 20 percent of your class at the most. However, these 20 percent will not learn what you are teaching if they are unable to comprehend what you are saying or writing. You can make it comprehensible with peer assistance or more simple language forms and vocabulary.

This is even more complicated when the ESOL student assumes that the other students understand everything even if they don't. When ESOL students get nervous about getting further behind, they do get further behind. For example, I was in a class one day when students were learning about intervals on a graph. I saw a look of concern on some of the ESOL students' faces. They didn't know what an interval was and thought that they should—these were advanced students! I asked the class what an interval is and the ESOL students seemed to relax when they realized that few of the other students raised their hands and only one really understood what it was. They relaxed because they realized that they weren't supposed to know what it was at that time.

Try to keep ESOL students at ease and feeling included by constantly reviewing essential concepts in simple English. It is also helpful to realize an ESOL student's differences in background knowledge when giving examples. Even a reference to the 9/11/2001 tragedies may not mean much to a newly arrived student from rural Guatemala, just as a reference to the 30-year civil war that recently ended in Guatemala would mean little to most students here at Otwell.

The last thing that I would like to share with you is how different each ESOL students is. Here are some examples. Try to guess which ESOL student I am referring to—it could be one or many:

- She came here in third grade, so she never really learned how to read Spanish. However, she's a good student, so her first language academically is actually English.

- He just moved here from a rural area of Mexico and is behind in Spanish and math. His parents both have a third grade education.

- He came from an urban area in Mexico and could afford to go to the best private school there. He has been here for three years, and his parents encourage him to learn his first language by reading it with him at home.

- Her parents want her to do well, and she is capable of it. However, the parents have limited education and both work until 9:00 p.m. They tell her that education is important, but she knows that survival and taking care of her siblings is more important to her family right now.

- She has been in the United States for four years, but has been in three different schools. She can speak and understand English and has acquired the survival skill of copying work to get good grades. However, she doesn't really know the content.

- He came here two years ago. His father's education is limited. He works hard, has acquired conversational English, is creative, and has been referred for Horizons (gifted) testing!

None of the above is an exact description of any individual student here as far as I know. However, any of the above may be in your class. If you have any questions about the background of an ESOL student, ask Alinee, Mary Ann, Andrea Thomas, Sally Campbell, Robin, me, or any of the student's former teachers. We may have some information that could help you or vice versa.

While we don't have all the resources that we would like for working with ESOL students, to be honest, what we do have is about as good as it gets. We are supported by the county and the school and by the great teachers here at Otwell. Let us help you when we can; we appreciate all you do for us in the ESOL department.

Have a great weekend!

Brent

27

Differentiation: Inconvenient but Inescapable

Teaching Them All

If all students at each grade level had identical or even similar intellectual capabilities, language skills, and family backgrounds, our jobs as educators would likely be a great deal easier. In reality, however, this is obviously not the case, and it becomes less so with each passing year. In order for any school to succeed, all teachers must commit to "teaching them all." Administrators must lead teachers in understanding that this is a requirement, not an option.

The following Friday Focus addressed an issue we hear more about each year in education: differentiation of instruction. Differentiation is no longer limited to certain special education students. Instead, it applies to our students with limited English proficiency and even our gifted students. In fact, in an ideal world, every child enrolled at school would have what only special education students currently are provided with: an Individualized Educational Plan (IEP). An IEP states in a clear and specific way what goals will be addressed in a given period of time. While it is certainly important to write and adhere to an IEP for all special needs children, in truth, this is what all of our students need. (I can already hear the groans from our special education case managers as I write these words!) While I acknowledge the huge amount of time that goes into writing IEPs and convening annual meetings to review IEPs, the idea of individualizing instruction for all learners is one worth exploring, since all learners arrive with widely variant needs and strengths.

The 27th Friday

Up until this point, only two of our three assistant administrators had penned a Friday Focus. The following edition was written by Suzanne Korngold, who, although she was a first-year assistant principal and new to our school, had earned unanimous respect among our teaching staff. At the end of her writing, she invited teachers to see her if they wanted any additional information; she was thrilled (as was I when she told me on this Friday afternoon) that several teachers immediately asked her for more resources. While Suzanne had never served as a building-level administrator before, she had held a variety of teaching and leadership roles throughout her 20-plus years in education. Nearly all of Suzanne's previous experience had been in the area of special education, making her an ideal candidate at our school to write about differentiation of instruction.

Although the primary topic of Suzanne's writing was obviously differentiation, she also reinforced many other important themes we had been discussing at our school, including assessment. She deftly made the point that the two are directly related: we differentiate instruction based on the assessments we administer in order to best meet the needs of all learners.

Friday Focus!

February 25

"That students differ may be inconvenient. But it is inescapable."
Researcher/reformer Theodore Sizer

Carol Ann Tomlinson is a renowned educational scholar and professor at the University of Virginia. She has written extensively on the topic of differentiating instruction to better meet the needs of students. Tomlinson (1999) states that three trends are central to the goal of effective curriculum and instruction for contemporary learners:

- Today's classrooms are more diverse than at any time in our past—and we are seeing only the early stages of the diversity that will increasingly typify schools. In the face of burgeoning diversity, it is increasingly clear that one-size-fits-all teaching will fit fewer and fewer students.

- We have a compelling need to learn to teach in more flexible and personalized ways.

- There will continue to be an escalating demand that the vast majority of students leave high school with high-level knowledge and skills. We need to move nearly all of our students from knowledge acquisition to knowledge creation.

In essence, teachers need to teach high-level curriculum in flexible ways to ensure that each learner is prepared for a fast-paced world, where problem solving, self-directions, reasoning skills, and enduring knowledge are requirements for successful participation in society. Teaching flexibly means teaching with student variance in mind. It is our reality that some students learn far more rapidly and deeply than the prescribed curriculum anticipates—and that some students learn much more slowly and with great difficulty.

At Otwell Middle School, we are also finding that flexibility is necessary due to the reality that some students don't speak the language of the textbook. Brent Agnew, our ESOL teacher, coteaches with Sally Campbell, our seventh grade science teacher, and together they deliver high-quality curriculum with high instructional flexibility. The students in their class are both challenged and supported—no matter what their learning needs may be. Another example is the deep awareness that Deborah Thornton, our eighth grade language arts teacher, has that some students need movement, music, or peer assistance while they learn. Her class also provides visual demonstrations for those who learn best through that modality, but she still provides for those who work more efficiently while still, in silence, alone, and from a book. Karen Pigott, in eighth grade social studies, uses the "think-pair-share" strategy for a deeper understanding of content knowledge and then "preview, midview, postview" for leading up to an assessment. Ronnie McNeese and Tony Collins, our sixth grade math teachers, effectively demonstrate flexible teaching by allowing one student to make connections with math by seeing it in building or construction and another student to make the same connection by seeing it in a sporting activity. They often model a "think-aloud" strategy to show students how they think about "what do I do first" to solve a problem, or they use choral responding so all students respond to the answer and receive immediate feedback. From this, you can see that flexible teaching is assessment driven: it responds to variance in student readiness, student interest, and student learning preferences.

The following chart (Tomlinson, 1999) explains what differentiation is and is not:

Differentiation Is	Differentiation Is Not
A way of thinking about and organizing teaching and learning.	A new idea or an instructional strategy.
All students exposed to key concepts, but at differing levels of complexity and depth.	Individualized instruction where every student is working on something entirely different.

Differentiation Is	Differentiation Is Not
Rooted in ongoing assessment and adjustment of curriculum.	A test at the end of each chapter to see who "got it."
The teacher guiding the exploration of a subject; the teacher as the coordinator of time, space, and materials.	The teacher as primary provider of information.
Learning organized around key concepts, themes, and common elements.	Fragmented teaching of unrelated skills.
Multiple approaches to content, process, and product designed to encourage maximal growth in all students.	One-size-fits-all instruction.
All students engaged in challenging tasks that produce high-quality work.	Giving some students "watered–down" tasks and others more of the same work to do.
Flexible grouping, including working alone, in pairs, in student-selected groups, in whole-class groups, and in cooperative groups.	A way to track students or make homogeneous groups.

Differentiation provides multiple approaches to content, process, and product. It requires that we adapt what we teach or how we give students access to what we want them to learn. It is also the way to a deeper understanding of the standards—what we want students to know, understand, and be able to do. Lastly, we hope it causes students to think about, apply, and expand the key understanding and skills of the standards being taught.

DuFour, DuFour, and Eaker's book *Whatever It Takes* (2004) suggests that educators must reflect on their current practices as well as look for strategies that might better meet the daunting, but vitally important, challenge of helping all students learn at high levels. Davenport and Anderson's book *Closing the Achievement Gap: No Excuses* (2002), one of my favorites, discusses how research shows that students attain the highest level of self-esteem when their teachers set a standard and expect them to meet that standard (even if it means bringing back the assignment three or four times and not letting them off the hook until the standard is met).

At Otwell Middle School, teams of teachers can work together to identify which students are least likely to meet state standards and why. Though well intended, do some of our current practices cause students to lose hope early on? What are some of those practices? As we continue our collaboration through professional learning communities, the answers to these questions will hopefully become more evident.

Everyone here at OMS believes that the academic potential of each student is tremendous. As a group, we must refuse to knuckle under to the difficult challenges that confront some students as excuses for poor learning. Knowing that one of the *greatest predictors of life success is educational success,* we must be committed to creating a school that knows no limits to the academic success of each student. I have a wealth of books and great websites on this topic; please feel free to see me if you are interested.

Enjoy your weekend.

Suzanne

28

Test Time

Like educators at all public schools in the nation, we are increasingly aware of the emphasis placed on standardized test results at the local, state, and federal levels. While we typically fare well on such state and national assessments at our school, we always struggle to meet or exceed standards in some areas, especially for certain student subgroup populations. Of course, the best way to ensure that schools perform well on annual assessments is not by "teaching to the test," but by hiring highly qualified teachers with exemplary human relations skills and establishing a climate and culture that allows them the opportunity to make the most of the instructional time allotted to them.

Having said that, as spring rolls around we do focus a bit more on all issues at our school related to testing. Certainly, we teach our students many tips for taking standardized tests. We expose them to practice tests not unlike the "real" ones they will take near the end of the school year. We identify students who are at risk for not meeting standards and provide them with additional support. One area that we have not spent a great deal of time on is writing valid test questions ourselves for use in creating our own formal assessments. As administrators, we ask that teachers of similar subject areas meet regularly and create common assessments. Since this is the case, it is important that the assessments they create effectively measure what it is we want students to learn.

The 28th Friday

The following Friday Focus was written by one of our veteran special education teachers, who was in the process of completing an advanced degree in educational leadership. I have found that having teachers on staff who are enrolled in graduate programs is extremely valuable. Such teachers not only broaden their own perspective and bring a great deal of new knowledge into their classrooms, they also are instrumental in spreading this knowledge to their colleagues. The author of this particular writing, Randi Sagona, is one of our finest teachers. She would also be wonderful as an administrator; luckily for me—and, more importantly, for her students—she insists on remaining in the classroom even today when she is sought-after as an administrative candidate in our system.

In her Friday Focus writing, Randi shared her expertise regarding what constitutes effective paper-and-pencil tests. In the past, teachers simply used tests provided by publishing companies or crafted hastily written tests of their own. Increasingly, our teachers are working together to devise tests that truly correlate with the standards being taught at each grade level within each subject area. Randi's tips below are practical, ring true, and were useful to us as we began writing more tests of our own as well as preparing students for the impending state-authorized standardized tests.

Friday Focus!

March 4

As many of you know, last summer I entered into the EdS program in teacher leadership at North Georgia College and State University. This semester, I have the pleasure of taking a class in data analysis with Dr. Judy Monsaas. Dr. Monsaas holds a PhD in measurement analysis and statistical evaluation. Her primary position is with the Board of Regents of the University System of Georgia, where she works on developing strategies for teaching and assessment in a standards-based environment.

During a recent class, Dr. Monsaas shared tips for writing good paper-and-pencil test questions. I found this session to be one of the most useful classes I have attended thus far, and am glad to be able to share some of this information with you. I pulled out the stuff that I found most enlightening, and I hope you find it as useful as I did! I should note that Dr. Monsaas indicated that the questions provided by textbook publishers in the form of test banks are not always as well-written as they should be. The following list is adapted from Linn and Grunland (2000) and contains tips for creating effective paper-and-pencil assessment questions of all types: true/false, matching, multiple choice, short answer/completion, and essay.

Tips for Writing Good Paper-and-Pencil Test Questions

There are several common barriers to students getting the correct answer (in other words, when the student knows the information, but gets it wrong anyway). These include the following:

- Excessive wordiness
- Difficult vocabulary
- Complex sentence structure

- Unclear illustrative material

True/False Questions

This type of question is used to measure students' ability to determine the correctness of a statement. It should be noted that many measurement specialists recommend against the use of true/false test items. An appropriate use of this format is to measure students' ability to distinguish fact from opinion.

Suggestions for writing true/false questions:

- Avoid broad statements.
- Avoid use of negative statements.
- Avoid long, complex sentences.
- Avoid including two ideas in one statement.

Matching

Matching items are appropriate for measuring factual information based on simple associations.

Suggestions for writing matching items:

- Use only homogeneous material in a single matching exercise.
- Include an unequal number of premises and responses; instruct the students that responses may be used more than once, not at all, etc.
- Arrange the list in logical order (dates, order characters appear in a novel, etc.).
- Place all items for matching exercises on one page.

Multiple Choice

Multiple-choice items are appropriate for measuring knowledge, understanding, and application (yes, they *can* get at higher-level thinking!).

Suggestions for writing multiple-choice items:

- The stem should include as much information as possible and should be free of irrelevant information (for example, "Base x height is the formula for _____" is a better stem than "What is the formula for the area of a rectangle?").
- Use negatively-stated stems only when outcome requires it (for example, "What should you NOT use to extinguish a grease fire?").
- An item should contain only one correct or clearly best answer—avoid using "A and B are both correct." Multiple-choice test

writers should also avoid "Which is the best..." questions, because they generally have more than one correct answer.

- All incorrect answers should be plausible. For instance, listing Brad Pitt as one of four choices for "Who was the fourth president of the United States?" only changes it to a three-choice question. If only three choices are to be offered, it should be written that way.

- Use "none of the above" or "all of the above" sparingly or not at all.

Short-Answer and Completion Items

These questions can be used for a wide variety of simple learning objectives.

Suggestions for writing short-answer items:

- Word items so the answer is brief and specific.

- A direct question is usually better than an incomplete statement.

- Do not take statements directly from textbooks as a basis for short-answer items.

Essay Questions

Essay questions should be used only for assessing higher-level thinking skills.

Suggestions for writing essay questions:

- Restrict the use of essay questions to those learning outcomes that cannot be measured satisfactorily by objective items.

- Phrase the question so that the student's task is clearly indicated.

- Indicate the approximate time limit for each question.

- Avoid the use of optional questions. Decide ahead of time what your objectives are and assess those. The use of optional questions implies that those topics are irrelevant.

Suggestions for scoring essays:

- Prepare an outline of the expected answer in advance.

- Decide how to handle factors that are irrelevant to the learning outcome being measured.

- When possible, evaluate the answers without looking at the student's name.

It is important to remember that we should strive for balanced assessments in our classrooms. Ideally, we will include performance assessments and portfolio assessments as we calculate our students' final grades. We will also include, of course, both formative and summative assessments in our courses. Inevitably, however, it remains the case—and perhaps rightly so—that a good deal of our assessments are of the old fashioned paper-and-pencil variety. In creating such assessments, I hope you will keep in mind the points shared above.

Have a great weekend!

Randi

29

PIRATES

At the time the following Friday Focus was sent out, the date of our all-important Georgia Criterion-Referenced Competency Tests was just over one month away. These are tests administered in the state of Georgia in grades 1 to 8 that determine whether or not a school makes Adequate Yearly Progress (AYP) under the NCLB initiative. The year before, our school had "made" AYP, but just barely, as we struggled to meet expectations across all student subgroups. This year, too, we knew that our results would place us just over or just below AYP minimum standards in certain categories. The previous week's Friday Focus set the stage for the theme of standardized testing by discussing how we can write better test questions ourselves; this week's topic directly related to improving student performance on standardized tests.

The 29th Friday

Although assistant principal Suzanne Korngold did not write her first Friday Focus until February, I asked her to write another one almost immediately for two reasons. First, I knew that she had gained a great deal of insight into how students can perform better on standardized testing through training she had received in another system. More importantly, Suzanne had the "E. F. Hutton" touch, that is, when she talked (or in this case, wrote), people listened. Both our students and teachers had grown to trust and respect this dynamic and solution-oriented educator.

I like to think that one reason all of our administrative team members work so well with teachers is because we are all teachers at heart. Currently, all of the administrators at our school had many years of successful teaching experience prior to entering the administrative arena. Having taught in core content areas for many years ourselves, we understand what good instruction looks like and what teachers need in terms of administrative support. One way we can support teachers is by sharing what we have learned over the course of our own teaching careers. Here, Suzanne shared a specific strategy that teachers could use in training students to improve their test scores.

You might think that the steps outlined below seem like simple, common-sense strategies that we already know. If so, you would be correct. Of course, we as educators are well-versed in how to take tests. In fact, if we ourselves were to take the tests we administer to students, we would probably achieve perfect or nearly perfect scores. However, we rarely take the time to pass on these commonsense strategies to our own students. The timing of the following writing was perfect for our situation. In the time remaining before our standardized test administration dates, teachers could spend just a short amount of time each day teaching their students the strategies Suzanne shared with them. I know that several of our teachers did just that—and we once again made AYP! While that accomplishment may not be attributable solely to the Friday Focus, I know that it helped some of our most at-risk students meet or exceed expectations on the tests they took that spring.

Friday Focus!

March 11

Test-taking skills *can* be learned—if you make it your business to teach them (Hughes, Schumaker, Deshler, Mercer, 1993).

PIRATES:

Prepare, **I**nspect, **R**ead, **A**nswer, **T**urn, **E**stimate, and **S**urvey

Research states that the majority of secondary students' course grades are derived from test scores. *The Test-Taking Strategy* (Hughes, Schumaker, Deshler, & Mercer, 1993) provides an effective and efficient way to markedly improve student performance on class-room tests. In 1990, when these strategies were prevalent at many schools, I jumped on the bandwagon and became trained in several of them. The PIRATES test-taking strategy was one of my favorite because it produced tangible results for students, parents, and teachers. I was teaching at Bair Middle School in Miami at the time, in a self-contained class for emotionally disturbed seventh and eighth graders. The students' emotional and behavioral needs dramatically affected their educational performance and mainstreaming capabilities. These were students whose tomfoolery (a Mr. Zoul word) would cause a substitute to pay off another substitute in order to switch classes. One time, a substitute actually walked out in the middle of the day, stating, "They told me they were special, not crazy." Taking tests only intensified their anxiety and tension in school—I guess I shouldn't have left a test on days I was out. Honestly, though, the PIRATES method did help my students increase their test scores by approximately 10 percent. Students who were receiving 70s on tests started making 80s. The test-taking strategy made them test-wise. Knowledge (gained through instruction and studying) plus "test-wiseness" equals good grades.

In most educational settings there are students who are low achievers. The causes vary, but in many instances it is because the students have not learned how to learn. The strategies promoted by Hughes and colleagues can teach students how to learn and how to perform tasks independently. They are designed to teach students to allocate time and order of importance to each section of the test, carefully read and focus on important elements in test instructions, and utilize other learning strategies. Although teachers must be trained in the PIRATES strategy (Hughes et al., 1993) for successful student mastery, following is an overview:

Step 1: **P**repare to succeed.

Step 2: **I**nspect the instructions.

Step 3: **R**ead, remember, and reduce.

Step 4: **A**nswer or abandon.

Step 5: **T**urn back.

Step 6: **E**stimate.

Step 7: **S**urvey.

Prepare to succeed means to allot time for all sections, scan the sections for length and difficulty, stay positive, and start within two minutes of when the teacher has passed out the test. Students should write "PIRATES" on the top of your paper to help them remember the steps.

Inspect the instructions means to **read** the instructions carefully, **underline** *what to do* and *where to respond,* and **notice** any special requirements. (Remember the mnemonic RUN.)

Read, remember, and reduce means to read the whole question and all choices given, remember what was studied, and then reduce the choices. Students should cross out the ones they know are not possible answers.

Answer or abandon means either answer it or move on to the next question. Students should not waste time on questions they are not sure of. Many times continuing on with the test may assist them in answering ones they originally had difficulty with.

Turn back simply means that at the end of the test, students should go back to any abandoned questions and answers. Unless it is a test that penalizes for wrong answers, they should answer **all** questions.

Estimate means students should make their best guess as to the right answer by remembering the **ACE** acronym: **a**void words such as "no," "always," "only," "none," "never," "every," and so on unless they definitely know the answer; **c**hoose the longest or most detailed choice; and **e**liminate similar choices.

Survey the entire test. Students should ensure all questions are answered and switch an answer only if they're sure about the answer.

During one of my drive-by visits to Ms. Sellen's math class, she taught me a new strategy. Ms. Sellen teaches her students to look at the answer choices before reading the question itself (for reading comprehension tests, students can just read the questions prior to reading the selection). By acting like "direction signs," the answers supply the brain with a frame of reference and start it on the path to the correct answer. It is a head start that may reduce students' levels of test stress and improve their level of success. Great thought, Ms. Sellen!

Teachers, thank you for teaching our students important content each and every day throughout the year. Thanks also for making time to periodically help our students perform better on standardized tests.

Happy Weekend!

Suzanne

Part 4

The Fourth Quarter

For the final stretch of the school year, as well as the final section of this book, our aim is multifaceted. First, we still want to focus on the present, teaching right up until the very last day of school and making the most of every learning opportunity. We also, however, want to reflect just a bit on what we have already accomplished throughout the year, reviewing what has worked and reminding ourselves of what areas still require our attention and need improvement. Even more important, perhaps, we begin to look ahead, ever so slightly, to the future. While we have many miles to go before we put another school year behind us, we can strategically use this time to set the stage for future learning opportunities during the next school year and beyond.

Of the eight Friday Focus writings included in this final section of the book, three were written by me. These included the final one, which celebrated the many accomplishments we achieved as a school throughout the year. While the fourth quarter of the school year is an appropriate time to look behind, look ahead, and remind ourselves of a few core values and best practices, it is not an ideal time to put forth a great number of new ideas for teachers to scrutinize and attempt to incorporate into their classrooms. Most of the topics that follow, therefore, do not offer specific teaching strategies or ideas for creating elaborate units of study. Instead, they focused on items of importance to our entire faculty, each of which is related to the school climate and school culture we worked hard to establish and cultivate throughout each week of the school year.

30

Professional Learning Communities

Soon after I began my tenure as principal of our school, we began examining our current school mission. Early on in our leadership team meetings, we decided that for the following year, creating a new mission, motto, and vision, along with faculty value statements, would be one of our priorities. We spent a fair amount of time learning about the purposes of mission, vision, value, and goal statements and how best to craft them throughout the school year so that we would be prepared to facilitate the adoption process early in the following school year. Although our value statements would be written only after gaining a consensus from all staff, I hoped that one of our adopted statements would refer to our commitment to ongoing professional development. In my experience, the very best schools are those that are staffed by teachers who are continuously trying to improve as professionals.

Context, Process, and Content

We are fortunate that our school system sets aside several days each year for professional development. My own experience with professional development opportunities has been mixed. While I am always excited about gaining practical new knowledge that I can then take back to my school and apply or share with others, nothing is more frustrating than sitting through an in-service session that has little or no relevance to what we do each day. As a basketball coach for many years, I used to enjoy attending coaching clinics. At these clinics, successful coaches from around the country would stand up and share specific strategies that had helped to make them successful. Whether these coaches were diagramming in-bounds plays, describing zone defenses, explaining their man-to-man defensive philosophy, or sharing drills they used in practice, I always found that these sharing sessions helped me as a coach by providing me with new ideas I could then try out for myself. As a principal, my goal is to provide similarly practical professional development opportunities for our teachers. Getting teachers to collaborate for the purpose of improving their practice and, ultimately, student learning is one of my primary areas of focus as a school administrator.

As a school principal interested in professional development, I familiarized myself with the National Staff Development Council (NSDC) and their 12 standards for staff development. These standards are organized into three areas: context, process, and content. The context standards address organizational support for professional learning. The process standards focus on how professional development topics are identified, designed, and delivered. Finally, the content standards identify the knowledge, skills, and attitudes necessary to attain high levels of learning for all students. Stated simply, "context" refers to the setting in which learning occurs, "process" refers to the "how" of professional learning, and "content" refers to the "what" of professional learning.

Of the three domains, I felt that we should first focus on the context in which our professional growth would occur. Just as I learned a great deal about coaching basketball from listening to other basketball coaches, I felt that teachers learn best from each other. We had a school staffed by teachers with a wealth of experience, skills, and capabilities. I wanted our teachers to share their knowledge and best practices with their colleagues. Too often, teaching becomes a profession marked by isolation. While I always strive to afford teachers a great deal of individual autonomy within their own classrooms, I insist that we collaborate, share, and observe each other teaching as a way to broaden our knowledge base and keep our minds open to finding better teaching strategies.

One way in which we were beginning to address the context in which we, as professionals, learned was through the creation of our professional learning communities. While I knew that this initiative would not be fully implemented until the next school year, we had already spread the word throughout our staff that creating small- and large-group professional learning communities would be the way we would conduct our business in the future. Many teachers were already meeting in small groups to answer the three critical questions that by now are second nature to all of our teachers: (1) What is it we want students to learn? (2) How will we know if they have learned it? and (3) How will we respond when students do not learn? Examining these questions and arriving at answers would encompass both the "what" and the "how" of our professional learning. Completing this work through our PLCs would be the setting in which we learned.

The 30th Friday

Beth Holder, the author of the following Friday Focus edition, is our sixth grade administrator and the coordinator for our in-school suspension program. Her FF writing clearly and powerfully stated the benefits gained from organizing teachers into professional learning communities and having them work on common goals. Although dealing with discipline issues is central to Beth's everyday duties and vitally important to our school, still more important is her knowledge relating to a wide variety of staff development issues. Beth has devoted a significant amount of time to keeping abreast of the latest trends and best practices for school leaders interested in providing high-quality professional development opportunities for teachers.

In addition to writing intelligently on the topic of staff development, much like Friday Focus authors before her, Beth showed her humor and personal side through her writing. Her reference near the end of this piece to "geezers or guppies" became fodder for a great deal of subsequent joking among our staff.

Friday Focus!

March 18

The most powerful forms of staff development occur in ongoing teams that meet on a regular basis, preferably several times a week, for the purposes of learning, joint lesson planning, and problem solving. (National Staff Development Council, 2001)

As an organizational arrangement, the professional learning community is seen as a powerful staff development approach and a potent strategy for school change and improvement (Hord, 1997). The Georgia Staff Development Council believes in "High Quality Professional Learning for Every Educator Every Day!" I'm sure many of us support this statement; however, the only way this will happen is if professional learning is embedded into our workdays. "In a results-oriented environment, principals and their staffs craft visions and establish goals. They use data to help determine the distance between the current status and the results they seek. They select strategies to close the gap to achieve the desired results" (Hirsch, 2002). Does this sound familiar? While we are engaging in our PLC group time, we are not only having an impact on our student learning, we are having an impact on our own professional development as well. Just think about all we've learned this year about the power of PLC groups. What difference does it make if a staff is communally organized? What results, if any, might be gained from this kind of arrangement? In an abbreviated report of student and staff outcomes where schools engage in PLCs, the following were noted as affecting teachers' professional development (Hord, 1997).

For staff, the following results have been observed:

- Powerful learning that defines good teaching and classroom practice and that creates new knowledge and beliefs about teaching and learners.
- Increased meaning and understanding of the content that teachers teach and the roles they play in helping all students achieve expectations.
- Higher likelihood that teachers will be well informed, professionally renewed, and inspired to inspire students.
- Significant advances in adapting teaching to the students, accomplished more quickly than in traditional schools.
- Commitment to making significant and lasting changes.
- For students, the results include the following:
- Lower rates of absenteeism (we were third in the most recent attendance report!).
- Increased learning that is distributed more equitably (common assessments).
- Greater academic gains in math, science, history, and reading than in traditional schools.
- Smaller achievement gaps between students from different backgrounds.

I have already learned tremendously from my own PLC group. Many of you would agree that your own learning during this time has been substantial. I feel that I have significantly improved in some areas already. My data analysis skills have certainly been honed. Going over and over the numbers has helped me tremendously, especially as a new member of the staff, to become more familiar with the learning profile of Otwell Middle School. I now have a greater knowledge of each subject area's strengths and weaknesses. I've also been able to zero in on some of our at-risk students and analyze the areas in which they need additional support. As we meet with teachers, both individually and in teams, I'm hearing that many of you are learning new teaching strategies and ideas from each other. In addition to creating common assessments, we are beginning to see the benefits of those common assessments. Earlier, we wrote our schoolwide goals for the year; I now believe that we are more clearly focused on those goals and have a clearer plan of how we are going to achieve them. Lastly, we've assessed ourselves on how well we differentiate our assessments and compared notes with our group members. Not only are we learning from others, but we are learning things about ourselves that are helping us become better at what we do. These are just a few areas where we are learning and improving through the work we do with PLCs. There are certainly more that we'll be able to add throughout this school year and beyond.

The following are the National Staff Development Council's standards for staff development (2001). The Georgia Staff Development Council recognizes and adheres to these standards. Take note of their very first standard, which addresses PLCs.

NSDC Standards for Staff Development

Context Standards

Staff development that improves the learning of all students

- organizes adults into learning communities whose goals are aligned with those of the school and district. (Learning Communities)
- requires skillful school and district leaders who guide continuous instructional improvement. (Leadership)
- requires resources to support adult learning and collaboration. (Resources)

Process Standards

Staff development that improves the learning of all students

- uses disaggregated student data to determine adult learning priorities, monitor progress, and help sustain continuous improvement. (Data-Driven)
- uses multiple sources of information to guide improvement and demonstrate its impact. (Evaluation)
- prepares educators to apply research to decision making. (Research-Based)
- uses learning strategies appropriate to the intended goal. (Design)
- applies knowledge about human learning and change. (Learning)
- provides educators with the knowledge and skills to collaborate. (Collaboration)

Content Standards

Staff development that improves the learning of all students

- prepares educators to understand and appreciate all students; create safe, orderly, and supportive learning environments; and hold high expectations for their academic achievement. (Equity)
- deepens educators' content knowledge, provides them with re-search-based instructional strategies to assist students in meeting rigorous academic standards, and prepares them to use various types of classroom assessments appropriately. (Quality Teaching)
- provides educators with knowledge and skills to involve families and other stakeholders appropriately. (Family Involvement)

We knew we were on track at Otwell, but in reviewing the National Staff Development Council's standards, it's certainly reaffirming to note that an organization filled with educational experts supports what we do! Not only are our students being positively affected as a result of our PLC work, but so is our own professional development. I am so excited to be part of a school where I can continue to grow as a professional. No matter what stage of our career we are in—geezer or guppy—there will always be room for more learning. That's why we are teachers; we love seeing our students learn, and we love to learn ourselves.

Happy Friday!

Beth

31

Choosing Positive

The 31st Friday

The following Friday Focus stood in stark contrast to the one immediately preceding it. While the former examined in an almost scholarly fashion an important component of teaching—ongoing professional development—this one addressed in simple language a much more mundane, but no less important topic: staff morale.

At the time of this writing, we were approaching our week of Spring Break. Once we returned from our break, it would not be too long before another year had ended. At this time of year, "spring fever" typically attacks many of our students, evidencing itself with a variety of symptoms. Teachers, too, are afflicted with this malady at times. Unfortunately, symptoms for some staff members may include the onset of complaining—about students, administrators, too many things going on at school, the upcoming standardized test administration, and a variety of other things that occur in schools each year at this time. This Friday Focus reminded us all of the influence we have on our students and what type of influence we want to be.

Amber Castleberry is a sixth grade language arts teacher at our school and the author of the following Friday Focus. Like many on our staff, Amber is a devout person; rather than begin her edition of our weekly memo with a scholarly quotation, she instead opened with a Biblical passage which neatly fit her theme for the week.

Throughout this book, I have bragged about the dedication and professionalism of the teaching staff at our school. However, we are all humans, prone to human traps, including complaining about one thing or another related to our jobs. While I can accept—and even expect—a certain amount of constructive criticism during the course of a school year, I cannot tolerate teachers who have adopted complaining as a way of life and who consistently present me with problems but never offer possible solutions to these problems. Amber's writing was a gentle and appropriate reminder to all teachers about our purpose and our impact as educators.

Friday Focus!

"Let no corrupt communications proceed out of your mouth, but that which is good to the use of edifying, that it may minister grace unto the hearers." Ephesians 4:29

As we approach the final weeks of the school year, it is easy for many teachers to get into that familiar habit of complaining and wishing that the year would end. I want to be the one who encourages you not to fall into that rut; if you already have, I want to be the one who encourages you to find a rope and climb out.

Each and every day our students need us. I often embrace the fact that I may be the only constant presence in my students' lives. *I make a choice each day that I want that presence to be a* positive, *constant factor.* I encourage you to do the same.

It is a great opportunity that we have to come to school and have an impact on students' lives from day to day. If we look at teaching as what it is—a huge responsibility—we will realize that it is not to be taken lightly. Sure, there are days when some students grate on your nerves. Sure, there are some students that you wouldn't necessarily want to take home with you. Sure, there are some students from whom you might want to run away if you saw them at Wal-Mart. But we didn't take on the enormous responsibility of teaching to avoid students. Instead, we became teachers because we care about kids.

Over the next few weeks, I encourage you to eat lunch with your students. Wow! It is amazing how much you can learn from them when they feel that you are interested in their lives. I encourage you to give them an "attaboy" or an "attagirl" any time you can. I encourage you to avoid complaining and keep showing how much you really care. When students feel that their teachers care about them, when they feel safe in our classes, optimal learning will occur.

We are all great teachers, yet we could all be even better. At this time of the school year, it is vitally important that we serve as a stable, constructive factor in our students' lives. Again, we may be the only constant factors they have—let us commit to being *positive* ones!

"One good teacher in a lifetime may sometimes change a delinquent into a solid citizen." Philip Wylie

That "one good teacher" referred to in the quote above might just be you; have a positively wonderful weekend!

Amber

32

Extraordinary Teachers

All educators who are serious about their profession have examined the characteristics of effective teachers at some point in their college studies or during their career. Often, professors or staff development facilitators will ask a room full of teachers their opinion as to what traits are essential for great teachers. Each time I run across such a list in my reading, I pore over the characteristics with interest. Of all the lists I have examined, the one I included for teachers to peruse in the following Friday Focus is my favorite and seems to capture the essence of what makes an effective teacher at any level, from elementary school through graduate school.

The number one trait included in the list, which we stress repeatedly at our school in many avenues of communication is passion. The term conjures up many meanings to us, but as it applies to successful teachers, I prefer the definition "boundless enthusiasm." At our school, we have many extraordinary teachers. Ironically, one of the extraordinary math teachers I am thinking of has almost nothing in common with one of the extraordinary science teachers who comes to mind—except for their boundless enthusiasm. Their enthusiasm truly knows no bounds. They will do whatever it takes to help a student, hone their skills, or assist a colleague. While some of our greatest teachers may be more creative than others or more adept at assessment techniques, all of them excel at possessing and exhibiting enthusiasm—both for their subject matter and for their students.

The 32nd Friday

This Friday Focus went out to our teachers on the morning before our week off for Spring Break. Rather than expose teachers to an esoteric teaching theory or new strategy, I simply chose to remind teachers of what has been identified through research studies as characteristics of extraordinary teachers. Although over 300 such traits have been identified according to the source I referenced, this extensive list could be condensed into just six traits. Each of these traits was stressed throughout the year, and I wanted to remind our great teachers that they had what it takes to be considered extraordinary in their profession.

Of course, just as in any school, not every teacher at OMS would be considered "extraordinary," either by their colleagues or by their students. Of these, some have the potential to become extraordinary, whereas a few, unfortunately, are destined to remain mediocre. The more teachers we get to the "extraordinary" stage, the better it is for our students and the more uncomfortable it becomes for those teachers who settle for mediocrity. Exposing teachers to excellence and what it entails is one way to validate the performance of our very best teachers, motivate those who are still striving to reach that status, and force our least effective teachers to reflect on their own behavior in comparison with their colleagues.

Friday Focus!

April 1

When I was an undergraduate, I once confided to a favorite professor that I was interested in becoming a teacher. He immediately responded, "And if you lose your passion for it, make a change. Promise?" I promised. (Granrose, 2001)

Two Fridays ago, Bruce Cambigue mentioned something to me about the great myths of successful teaching as a potential Friday Focus topic. My curiosity was piqued by his reference, and I asked him about it. Bruce shared with me the book in which the above quote appears, *Extraordinary Teachers,* edited by Dr. Fred Stephenson (2001). I was going to steal the "great myths" theme as my FF topic, but in poring through this rich text, I was pulled to thievery of a different idea. Perhaps a future FF author will be moved to finally get to the "great myths of teaching" topic, but I was struck instead by a list of characteristics possessed by extraordinary teachers, and in particular by the number of references to "passion" as a must-have for effective teaching.

In the introductory chapter, Stephenson indicates that through research, he has identified more than 300 different traits that distinguish excellent teachers. He condenses these into six key characteristics of extraordinary teachers (I particularly identified with characteristic #1):

1. Extraordinary teachers have great **passion** for their work.

   Preeminent (Otwell Middle School) teachers are passionate about their subject matter, their students, learning, and teaching. They feel responsible, even obligated, to help *all* students. They want to share the thrill of discovery with their students. They wear the title of "teacher" with pride; finding their work exciting and meaningful is the chief driving force that motivates them to succeed.

2. Extraordinary teachers **know** what to teach, how to teach, and how to improve.

   Exemplary (Otwell Middle School) teachers see their primary task as preparing their students for life. An ultimate goal is to produce honorable and productive members of society. They have a craftsman's ability to choose the best tools for each particular task. They use their research knowledge as a powerful source of energy for both teaching and student learning. Top teachers will look anywhere and everywhere for help. They have the courage to accept risks and defy conventional wisdom.

3. Extraordinary teachers excel at creating **exciting** classroom environments.

   Exceptional (Otwell Middle School) teachers capture student interest with boundless energy and enthusiasm. Outstanding teachers grasp the importance of the first classroom meeting. They realize that by the time day one is over, most students will have already formed opinions about a teacher's interest in teaching them, whether the teacher wants to be there, if the instructor has passion for his or her field, and whether the teacher likes students. As a result, extraordinary teachers seize the opportunity to set a positive tone for the entire course during the first class session. Top teachers are cheerful individuals; their classroom is their stage and they relish the opportunity to perform for their students—not necessarily for laughs or popularity, but to excite a student response toward learning.

4. Extraordinary teachers **connect** exceptionally well with students.

   Highly effective (Otwell Middle School) teachers have an uncanny ability to connect with students. They get students to trust them, to be more receptive to their advice, and to believe in what they are trying to accomplish. Their goal is to create a bond, an educational partnership, with their students. They know that understanding, acceptance, compassion, and fairness carry much weight with children. They comprehend the importance of a teacher's character and credibility and try to be good role models.

5. Extraordinary teachers **challenge** students to reach their full potential.

   Outstanding (Otwell Middle School) teachers are demanding instructors who teach rigorous courses. Students are worked hard and held responsible for finishing assignments on time and for delivering quality performances. Such teachers have high standards, which are not compromised. Their motto seems to be, "I welcome any and all to my classes, but don't sign up unless you are serious about learning." Despite the widespread knowledge among students of the academic rigors that lie ahead, students flock to get into extraordinary teachers' classes.

6. Extraordinary teachers get extraordinary **results**.

   The ultimate characteristic of acclaimed (Otwell Middle School) teachers is that they get results that far exceed the teaching norm. These teachers receive accolades from students, colleagues, and parents. Their students perform well, year in and year out, despite the fluctuations in student ability levels. Top teachers teach students many more things than other teachers. They reach a greater number of students than other teachers. Excellent teachers change the way students approach and value education. They influence attitudes and behaviors. They open minds and hearts and help students find direction, meaning, and satisfaction in their lives.

Otwell teachers are indeed extraordinary. Thank you all for striving each day to demonstrate what preeminent, exemplary, exceptional, highly effective, outstanding, and acclaimed teachers do. We are truly a tight-knit family of teachers, and we learn from one another how to become even more proficient in our craft. At OMS, teachers are extraordinary because we *Teach with Passion* each day!

Have a glorious Spring Break; I will miss seeing you each day. Until the 11th, then, cheers!

Jeff

33

Making the Connection

At any given point in time during the year, our school calendar is likely to have on its schedule a variety of club meetings, activities, athletic events, performances, fund-raising drives, philanthropic endeavors, and field trips. Periodically, I worry that we may be taking our eye off the ball and not focusing on our primary business, which is academic achievement in the core areas of language arts, science, math, and social studies. Yet in observing our students—and our teachers—as they engage in and sponsor such activities, I know that these "extras" add to, rather than detract from, our ultimate goal of academic success for all.

At the middle school level, the word "connections" takes on great importance. In our classrooms, we want our students to make connections between what they are learning on a certain day in one course of study to material they learned previously in that course. We also want them to connect learning they acquire in one class to learning they gather in another discipline. Finally, we want students to connect new knowledge gained in classrooms to the world outside the schoolhouse and to their own lives. As a school, we want students to feel connected to the school community. Students who are involved in extracurricular activities are more likely to feel such a connection. As they transition from middle school to high school, the connection between the two is strengthened if they are involved in an activity at the middle grades level that is also offered at the high school level.

When I first began teaching middle school, students at our school took four core classes and two "exploratory" classes. Now we call these "Connections" classes, as each of them in some way connects to learning that is occurring in the core content areas.

The 33rd Friday

We have 10 Connections teachers at our school. Although they are all stellar teachers, I called on a first-year teacher at our school—our band teacher, Catherine Keyser—to write a Friday Focus that described the purpose and importance of the Connections classes. Catherine is simply one of the most masterful teachers with whom I have ever worked . She is petite in physical stature, but a giant in the eyes of her students. Catherine is a vivid example of a belief I hold to firmly that great teachers are great regardless of what they teach. For example, our very best first grade teachers could make the transition to middle school almost effortlessly. On the other hand, ineffective teachers are likely to remain ineffective no matter what they teach or at what grade level. A poor high school teacher is likely to perform poorly at the middle school level also.

Catherine, an accomplished musician, has never taught in a core content area, but having observed her teaching band to a room filled with nearly 100 sixth grade band students on numerous occasions, I'm convinced that she could begin teaching high school calculus tomorrow and perform admirably. In the following Friday Focus, Catherine spoke for her entire department in letting the rest of us see how the learning that was occurring in their area of the school connects with the curriculum and objectives within the core academic setting.

Friday Focus!

April 15

"Imagination is more important than knowledge. Knowledge is limited. Imagination encircles the world." Albert Einstein

"Why do we have to do this?" Any student at some time

How Do We Make It All Connect?

A few years ago in our little wing of the school, we were the "exploratory" classes, the purpose of which was to provide a place where students could explore areas of interest outside the basic core subjects. Now we are "Connections" classes, and while students still explore other areas of interest, part of the purpose of our classes is to connect to the basic core subjects of language arts, math, science, and social studies. When kids ask, "Why do we have to know this?" we can often help provide that answer. We have national standards and curriculum expectations for our various fields, and some disciplines allow more opportunity to connect to academics than others. However, the Connections classes help the students apply what they are learning in the core areas and take their learning a step further. Here are a few examples of how we incorporate the academic curriculum into our classes:

Art

Mrs. Dareing's students produce beautiful work; check out the still-life charcoals they just finished!

- Every unit begins with a reading and writing assignment.
- Students use compasses and rulers to conceptualize spatial relationships.
- Students learn about African art, which corresponds with the seventh grade social studies curriculum.

Technology

Have you seen some of the cool things Mr. Z.'s kids are making?

- Students apply the laws of physics by building bridges and racing cars.
- Students apply their math skills on a regular basis. For example, some of the students are constructing a townhome (it is absolutely unreal what these kids did by hand).
- Language arts skills are reinforced through writing assignments.

Computer Literacy

Mrs. Richardson's classes are always creating projects based on their academics while learning to use various computer programs. Students in her class

- produce poetry and improve letter writing.
- create websites for environmental and animal science studies.
- review and diagram the parts of speech.

For those of us whose classes are based more on physical performance, tying into the academic curriculum is more challenging. Our students must show a physical or audible difference from the beginning to the end of the nine-week grading period:

Health and P.E.

- Students understand the importance of physical activity and health as it relates to their daily lives.
- Teachers incorporate science vocabulary in the health and P.E. classes as students learn how the body functions and how to take care of it.
- P.E. also covers physical science vocabulary as it applies to various sports.

Niyelo

- Students learn to set goals and expectations for themselves and their group. In the process, they learn valuable life and social skills.

Performing Arts

- We work to instill in our students the importance of organization, dedication, and creativity.

In my brief experience, I have found that sometimes students who are unsuccessful in academic areas can be outstanding achievers in the Connections classes. Some of my best musicians have been students who are mildly autistic or who have Asperger Syndrome. A former colleague could pull the most beautiful oil paintings out of kids who had emotional or behavioral disorders. We all know why what we are teaching is important; getting the students to also understand why is one of our greatest challenges.

To my Connections teammates, thank you for your awesome support. I hope you'll forgive my exploitations of your programs. To my friends in the academic areas, thanks for recognizing that what we do in Connections relates directly back to what you are teaching. Together, we enrich the learning experiences of our students.

Happy Friday!

Catherine

34

"I" Messages

With only a few weeks left in the school year, our students—and sometimes even our teachers—tend to succumb to the temptation of slacking off. There could not be a worse time to do so. While it is true that our standardized testing was completed a week earlier and the vast majority of the various curriculum standards at each grade level and within each discipline had been taught, we still had three full weeks of student school days remaining. Too often, we have a tendency to ease up at the most inopportune time: just before the finish line.

Clearly, as I have suggested earlier in this book, the first day of the school year is one of the most important. This day sets the stage for all that is to follow. Students leave each teacher's classroom on that first day having already formed an opinion of the course and the instructor that is unlikely to change dramatically one way or the other in subsequent days. The final days of the school year are similarly important. Students can leave for the summer with a good feeling about what they have learned and accomplished, or they can leave with a sour taste for what has occurred, perhaps only because of a negative incident or two right at the end of the year. Such incidents can erase many more positive ones that happened regularly earlier on.

Whether our students are leaving us only for the summer and returning in the fall, or whether they are leaving us for good as they climb the next rung of the educational ladder into high school, we want them leaving with a sense of accomplishment and a feeling that they have worked hard and had fun doing so throughout the year. When students misbehave at this time of the school year, teachers must take care to react appropriately, just as they would at any other time of the year. In so doing, it is important that we condemn the behavior, not the student who is exhibiting the behavior.

The 34th Friday

For this Friday Focus, I once again called on our assistant principal, Suzanne Korngold. This is the third and final Friday Focus that Suzanne wrote during the course of the school year. Other than myself, Suzanne was the only staff member who contributed more than one edition of our weekly teaching and learning communication. As I mentioned in Chapter 29, this was due to her vast expertise as well as the respect she had earned among the teachers at our school. As always, she wrote powerfully and provided teachers with specific strategies they could try themselves in working with students. In addition, as is her wont, she managed to poke fun of me in making her point!

For her final Friday Focus writing, Suzanne drew on her primary area of expertise and experience: dealing with students who have a tendency to misbehave. She shared with teachers a strategy she has implemented successfully in correcting student behavior indiscretions. Through the use of "I" messages, Suzanne suggested that we let students know it is not that their behavior is bothering us, but that the consequences of their behavior is the true cause of our concern. As we moved into the homestretch of the school year, the wisdom she shared was most appropriate.

Friday Focus!

April 22

"Say what you mean, mean what you say, but don't say it mean."
BASSS motto

Serving in the Broward County School District as an area behavior program specialist came with extensive job responsibilities. In the fifth largest fully accredited school district in the United States, the special education population was immense and diverse. One of my roles was assisting schools with behavior intervention plans and classroom management strategies. Along with a team of 12 support teachers, I developed a workshop geared toward increasing positive behavior and enhancing curriculum. The workshop, designed primarily for special education teachers, was also highly recommended for regular education teachers who taught inclusion classes. The workshop was called **B**ehavioral and **A**cademic **S**trategies for **S**tudent **S**uccess (BASSS).

The BASSS manual covered curriculum strategies as well as positive behavioral strategies for teachers to use in their classroom. One of my favorite sections of the workshop to teach focused on effective communication through the use of "I" messages. In the book Cooperative Discipline (Albert & DeSisto, 1995), the authors discuss the importance of "open vs. closed" communication and the use of "I messages" as an effective communication tool in the classroom. They strongly suggest that it is usually not the student's behavior that is displeasing you as the teacher, but rather the consequences the behavior produces for you and how it interferes with your needs or rights. If the student's behavior did not produce these consequences, you would probably not be bothered by it (unless it was harmful or dangerous).

Effective communication is a skill that can be learned and practiced. "I" messages are most helpful when you have a problem with a student or person based on his or her behavior. There are three parts to an "I" message:

- Describe the behavior ("Running in the classroom...").
- State your feelings about the behavior ("...makes me feel annoyed...").
- State the consequences of the behavior ("...because it disrupts the other students and someone could get hurt.").

"I" messages are effective because

- they place responsibility with the sender of the message.
- they reduce the other person's defensiveness and resistance to further communication.
- they provide information about the other person's behavior but do not evaluate it.
- they help promote open communication in work and personal relationships.
- they build trust, create empathy, and facilitate understanding between sender and receiver.

When you are not describing your own feelings as you send a message, you may be evaluating, ordering, or blaming the other person. When you are blaming someone else, you are sending "you" messages that may result in ineffective communication.

Here is an activity for you to demonstrate the practical use of "I" messages:

- You are doing a presentation on sea life in your classroom, and a group of students is talking excessively. Their behavior is interfering with your presentation; you feel displeased because you cannot teach.

Is it the students' behavior (excessive talking) that is disturbing you, or is it the consequences their behavior has for you? Obviously, the disturbing element is the frustration the consequences their behavior holds for you. Therefore, when you tell the students how you feel about their behavior, let them know that your feelings relate to the consequences of their behavior, rather than the behavior itself. "With all the noise this group is making, I'm having a difficult time teaching the rest of the class." Try these two yourselves:

- You keep snacks in your desk to eat at school. Your principal regularly helps himself to these without asking, often consuming all of them. (If you don't yet know, Mr. Zoul has the propensity to pilfer others' edibles, whether in front of them or behind their back. Please choose your words wisely on this one.)

- A student has not returned a math book that was loaned to him over a week ago.

How did you do? Were you able to respond according to the guidelines shared above? This form of communication identifies the behavior of concern, not the individual. Students (and principals!) are more likely to accept ownership of their behavior when it is not addressed in a blaming or attacking way. The most important things to remember about "I" messages are that they focus on you, not on the students, and that they do not place blame on anyone.

As we move through these final weeks of school, our students' behaviors may well frustrate us. Thanks for thinking about how best to respond if and when this occurs.

Happy Friday!

Suzanne

35

Teaching People, Not Content

With only a few weeks remaining in the school year, there was still so much I wanted to share with our teachers. Of course, the end of the school year is not the optimal time to introduce teachers to new ideas we would like them to implement in their classrooms. Obviously, most teachers are not receptive to such insights at this time. Although I did not feel this was a time to write about something completely new, it did seem like an appropriate time to revisit the work of Rich Allen's *Impact Teaching* (2002), a work that many of our teachers were familiar with and whose philosophy mirrors much of what we write about in this book.

The 35th Friday

Allen (2002) examines how teachers can maximize their impact on students in the limited time they have together during the course of a school year. Although he provides many specific strategies that teachers at our school had incorporated into daily practice, it is his philosophy as much as his learning strategies that I find most appealing. The following Friday Focus highlighted the perspective that, as educators, we should concentrate on teaching *people* instead of *content*. Much of what we have written about in this book relates directly to this theme. We are and always will be in the people business. No matter how passionate we are about our subject matter, we must be even more enthusiastic about our students. It matters not if we have the newest and most innovative programs if we do not first have inspired people putting them to good use. Even our standardized tests are of limited value in that they only measure facts that our students have memorized and not the life lessons we have taught them.

At this point in the school year, it seemed logical to remind our teachers of this noble perspective: that our school is filled with genuine people first, people who happen to be students and teachers during the hours they are in our school together. While my primary goal was to remind teachers of this philosophy, I also wanted to make a few last-minute suggestions. In particular, during my walks through the school each day during this particular week, I had noticed more students in the hallways than usual. Too often, it seemed to me, teachers were allowing the entire class to take a "restroom break" just for the sake of taking a break. As I mentioned in the previous chapter, there is no worse time to take our eye off the ball than with mere days remaining in the school year. The advice I offered regarding allowing student "breaks" in the middle of a class is advice I would strongly encourage all teachers to follow from the very first day of school until the very final day of school.

As was my general practice, I began the Friday Focus with a brief personal anecdote from my own teaching career many years ago. The relationship between principal and teacher is not wholly unlike the teacher-student relationship. Just as the quote implies, people want to know that you care about them. This is as true for the student learning from a teacher as it is for the teacher working with an administrator. I encourage my teachers to teach students not only the content-area material but also about who they are as teachers and, more importantly, as human beings. By beginning my Friday Focus writings with short personal experiences, I shared just a bit of my own teaching expertise and a whole lot more about who I am as a person. At this time in the school year, we must remember that we are teaching people, not just content.

Friday Focus!

April 29

The ultimate goal of classroom teachers is to have a significant impact on the students, an impact that results in a measurable increase in students' knowledge or skills. (Allen, 2002)

"Students want to know how much we care before they care how much we know."

The second quote above is one that you have likely heard before. I first heard this and took it to heart during my sixth year of teaching. I was teaching eighth grade language arts in Gwinnett County. Our principal was Judi Rogers, whose husband was then–state superintendent Werner Rogers. I always felt that it was somewhat advantageous to our school having this connection, as Superintendent Rogers often visited with us. During one such visit to my classroom, he shared this quote with me when he noticed my "Quote du Jour" on the board. Many of you are also likely familiar with Rich Allen, responsible for the first quote above, who has visited with several Forsyth County schools. Allen (2002) writes about what he calls "impact teaching,"offering five tenets concerning the nature of effective instruction:

- Teach people, not content.
- Awareness leads to choice.
- Learning + enjoyment = retention.
- Application is everything.
- Stories are great.

Each of these precepts is one with which I concur. The first one—teaching people, not content—holds special meaning for me.

While not wishing to sound thrasonical, no one is more passionate about their subject matter than I, yet I know that passion for my subject matter is meaningless if I am not passionate about my students. I have many friends who teach high school and who are truly master teachers. One reason I value middle school teachers, however, is directly related to this concept. Too often, high school teachers emphasize teaching content, not students. Otwell Middle School stands as an exemplar for the reverse, and I thank you all for that.

How can we live this mission? First, we must realize that all learners are truly unique. We must get to know each individual learner as the year progresses in order to best serve them. Also, although we all feel pressure to "cover" a vast curriculum, it is important to remember the "teachable moments" that naturally arise during the year—those moments that deviate from the lesson or even the curriculum, but which will be infinitely more valuable to students and the learning environment in the long run. It is not only okay, but advisable, to cherish such moments in order to teach our kids a life lesson and allow for more productive learning later.

Another example of teaching people is the issue of allowing "breaks." In the middle of a lesson, it may become apparent that the group needs a break. If no instructional strategy can be found to keep the lesson presentation useful, then it is probably best to honor the needs of the group and take a quick break or even a simple "stand up and stretch" moment. I have found in my own experience that breaks are most useful if they are taken when needed, not as a regularly scheduled event.

Getting to know each student's interests outside of class is another way of honoring the "teach people, not content" philosophy. So many of you do this by learning of your students' interests, sponsoring clubs, and attending their after-school events. In addition, effective teachers often teach with students, not to students. Create an environment in which all members of the group work together to learn material. Finally, having a sense of humor and letting students know you value fun as a logical companion to hard work is another way of making it obvious that you teach people, not merely content.

Curriculum content is of utmost importance and is our core business. However, if the needs of the group are interfering with learning the aforementioned content, these needs must be addressed. Responding immediately to the needs of the group or an individual will allow for enhanced concentration at a subsequent point. Thanks for knowing inherently that our students are people first and for respecting their needs as unique learners. Teaching people, not content, is another way we *Teach with Passion* each day!

Have an awesome weekend!

Jeff

36

My Parents' Expectations

The 36th Friday

For the next-to-last Friday Focus of the year, I called on Deborah Thornton to write on a topic of her own choosing. Deborah, one of our finest language arts teachers, came to the teaching profession later in life than most teachers at our school. Her classroom is one of the warmest and most inviting classrooms I have ever set foot in (the Friday Focus in Chapter 27 alludes to her various skills). In many ways, I consider Deborah a "traditional" teacher. For example, she is very adamant that all students conform to her very strict behavioral expectations. She also places a great amount of emphasis in her eighth grade language arts class on "old-fashioned" skills such as grammar (I've even known her to diagram sentences with her students!). She is also traditional, perhaps, in the fact that she currently lives and teaches in the same small city in which she was raised. On the other hand, I also consider Deborah to be one of our most innovative and open-minded teachers. Although she is a traditionalist in many ways, her use of music and soft lighting suggests another side of her as a teacher. More significantly, she had attended a workshop not long before this Friday Focus was written and returned to tell me that beginning in the fall she would be completely changing her approach to teaching, adopting a "workshop" approach to teaching both reading and writing.

In her Friday Focus, we got a sense of both Deborah Thornton the traditionalist and Deborah Thornton the innovator. She wrote about her parents and how they inspired her to succeed simply by maintaining high expectations for her and her siblings. In the very first chapter of this book, I wrote about my two nonnegotiable components of effective teaching: expectations and relationships. Here, Deborah—unwittingly, I'm sure—took us full circle by once again stressing how establishing high expectations can set the stage for success. Although Deborah herself was reared by "traditional" parents, she reminded us that times have changed and that we, as educators, may need to assume the role of parent—to some extent—for many of our students.

Deborah makes reference to "GPS" in her Friday Focus. GPS stands for "Georgia Performance Standards," the new curriculum adopted in our state that was being phased in at schools in Georgia during the following school year. It will be fully implemented in all subject areas and grade levels by 2008. Not surprisingly, rolling out a new curriculum and having to learn all that goes along with such an enormous change was causing a certain amount of angst on the part of some teachers. While I sense just the tiniest bit of rebellion in her tone as she talks about rolling out the new curriculum in her classroom next year, I know that she is a consummate professional and will likely lead others in absorbing and teaching the new language arts curriculum. Even so, while she adapts to yet another change in education and incorporates that change into her own classroom, it is clear that she will hold onto the tried-and-true teachings of what she calls "MPE."

With only a week to go in the school year, the following writing was a lighthearted approach to a serious topic. Its timeliness and wit were appreciated by our teachers.

Friday Focus!

May 6

"Education is what survives when what has been learned has been forgotten." B. F. Skinner

Before there was GPS, there was MPE. MPE is different than GPS in that it has nothing to do with curriculum or expectations for teachers. No, MPE—"My Parents' Expectations"—focuses entirely on providing a foundation that will guarantee achievement in every area of a child's life; these expectations include, but are not limited to, education. Often, MPE statements are clichés that, once recycled into the lives of the young, become the tenets, along with those of their religious faith, that undergird their lives. Such was the case with me.

For example, "*Can't* never could do anything," was my daddy's MPE response every time we whined—usually any time something was, or even gave the appearance that it might be, a little difficult. "Now, get busy" always concluded his *Can't* declaration. Long before I understood the logic of the first part, the "get busy" directive was ingrained in me as habit. In this way, Daddy's use of MPE developed independence and the ability to self-start in my four siblings and me. (This was such a powerful MPE that Nike recycled the cliché years later—without even bothering to gain Daddy's permission—and adopted it as their "Just Do It" slogan.)

Then, there was the "Do your best, work hard, and you can achieve anything you want" MPE mantra in our home. No one was excused from working hard or giving less than his or her very best effort at all times. From experience, my parents knew that adolescence was the training ground for life, so we had chores at home, part-time jobs at an early age, As in school, and hordes of extracurricular activities in which to participate. My parents understood how easily society allows individuals to settle for the least that life has to offer; they had shunned the perfect opportunity to do so, and they pushed us to do the same.

Mama and Daddy didn't just teach this MPE; they lived it. Married at 16, they had four children by the time they were 20. With little support or positive influence, they could have easily justified providing the minimum for their children. Instead, Daddy spent the rest of his "growing-up" years working 50 or more hours each week. While doing so, he never missed a ballgame or other important event in any of our lives. He found the time, somehow, not only to carry us on nature walks and tell us stories about his youth, but also to share his dreams, which inspired us to dream, too. At home, Mama constantly read and played games with us, helped us with our homework, and made sure, though money was scarce, that we got those "little extras" we craved at least once in a while. Mama also carpooled us, along with our friends, all over the county for ballgames, took us to plays in Atlanta, and through books, music, and poetry, showed us that there was a world beyond this place known as Cumming, Georgia. Their MPE modeling taught us that no adversity in life had to define us if we didn't allow it to do so. We could choose our perspective and our reaction to other people's perspectives—we alone were responsible for the outcomes of our own lives, not anyone else.

Lastly, the MPE "Get an education" refrain was so often repeated that I was well into school before I realized that the three words could be used separately. Ahead of their time in their advocacy for higher education, my parents promoted college not as an option, but as *the* option. Though they rarely wasted time or energy on the disappointments in their lives, both my parents grieved over their lack of education. GED recipients themselves, they stressed education as the road to all the opportunities that they wanted for us and that we would eventually want for ourselves. While my siblings and I all attained different levels of formal education, each of us continues to grow and use education to achieve what we desire in life.

Only with age and the passing years have I truly realized the gift that my parents were to their children or the gifts that they gave to me in the form of MPE statements. Only in retrospect have I understood that MPE wasn't just about values, discipline, succeeding in life, and expectations; MPE was a gift of love—a love that cared enough to hold itself responsible for not only teaching life lessons, but holding me accountable when I gave excuses instead of my best. So as I roll out the GPS in my classroom next year, I'm going to make sure that I roll out the MPE, too. For those students who haven't been exposed to the MPE, it might make all the difference in the GPS.

Deborah

37

A Culture of Success

We had come a long way as a staff and as a school from the time the first Friday Focus was written in August 2004 to May 13, 2005, when the following edition was distributed. In addition to making great strides in many areas related to teaching and learning in the current school year, we had set the stage for making even further progress in the coming year. Teachers on our staff and other administrators within our system had enjoyed the weekly communications written by me and other leaders at our school. Many of us were already looking forward to carrying this new tradition into its second year of existence beginning in the fall. For now, however, most of our teachers were simply looking forward to their summer vacation; another school year had slipped away from us, but not without many victories, both great and small.

Recognizing and Celebrating Success

At our school, we have several long-standing student and teacher recognition programs, as well as several brand-new ones. Each month, we recognize approximately 20 students as our "Shining Stars" for the month. They enjoy a pizza luncheon in the media center, at which they receive pins and certificates. Each quarter, we recognize our leading student readers—those students who earn the most points as recorded with the Accelerated Reader program. The top 25 point-earners receive a gift certificate to a local bookstore. The teacher whose class reads the most books also receives a gift certificate.

At our faculty meetings, we always recognize teachers with perfect attendance for the month; a few lucky winners are drawn at random to receive gift certificates to local stores or restaurants. At the end of each faculty meeting, we allow teachers to recognize each other for going the extra mile on behalf of a student or colleague. These are our "FISH" awards, which we instituted after reading *FISH! A Remarkable Way to Boost Morale and Improve Results* (Lundin, Paul, & Christensen, 2000). The award itself is none too exciting (a bag of Pepperidge Farm goldfish crackers and a bag of Swedish Fish candy), but these are some of my very favorite celebrations, as I watch teachers praise each other for making a difference at our school. On a quarterly basis, we also recognize a teacher for standing as a shining example of a person who lives our school's mission each and every day. We present the honoree with a nice plaque, accompanied, typically, with a slide presentation showing the teacher in action at our school. Finally, like most other schools, we annually select a Teacher of the Year. This year's recipient was Ronnie McNeese, a sixth grade math teacher and our football coach. Ronnie went on to win the award for our entire county.

In addition to the above celebrations, each quarter, teachers nominate six students at each grade level to receive our PRIDE awards. These go to our students who displayed all-around excellence throughout the quarter. At the PRIDE ceremonies we host each quarter, student honorees and their parents are invited to a breakfast at which the students receive a trophy and a nice certificate. We take their photos and post them in a prominent display case in our front lobby for the duration of the subsequent quarter. We also invite a guest speaker to say a few words at our PRIDE ceremonies. One speaker's words were used as the subject matter for our final Friday Focus.

At our school, I still make announcements each morning over the intercom. After reading whatever it is that we have in the way of announcements each morning, I close by imploring our students to "Work hard and have fun today." I am a firm believer that these two go hand in hand and that it is almost impossible to have fun if you have not also worked hard. Our students and our teachers had worked hard this year; it was important to recognize and celebrate their many successes throughout the year, especially as we brought yet another year to a close.

The 37th—and Final—Friday

The final Friday Focus of the school year was something I had written after our fourth-quarter PRIDE ceremony honoring some of our most outstanding students. I was still searching for a Friday Focus topic at the time, so I was delighted when one of my educational heroes and our former associate superintendent, Dr. Ellen Cohan, stood up and began speaking to the students and parents assembled in our cafeteria that morning. I immediately knew that I was hearing profound words of wisdom that I could steal and include in my final Friday Focus memo.

Dr. Cohan shared a list of eight simple characteristics of successful people, which she had come across in her own reading not long before. In listening to her share these with our students and parents, I felt a sense of pride, myself, in that much of what she was sharing as hallmarks of success were topics that we as a school had shared with each other throughout the year in our weekly Friday Focus writings. Much of what it takes to improve our schools can only be learned after years of study and even more years of experience. A great deal more, however, can be learned at a much earlier time and much more swiftly by recognizing what successful people in our world do each day in all walks of life. Successful teachers do this, too, and they lead their students to follow them on their path to success.

Friday Focus!

May 13

"Let each become all that he was created capable of being."
Thomas Carlyle

"Our strength, creativity, and growth as a society depend upon our capacity to develop the talents and potentialities of our people."
John Gardner

Famous quotations related to the theme of success are in abundant supply; the two above are but two among thousands. In closing yet another school year, it is important to remind ourselves that we are in the business of success. Our core business is to ensure the success of all students who enter through our portals each day. Of course, one cannot ensure the success of others without being a person of success oneself. The single greatest factor that contributes to the success of Otwell Middle School is the fact that we are staffed by eminently successful teachers. Not a day passes without my quietly and thankfully reflecting on my good fortune in working at a school filled with such successful adults.

At our final PRIDE ceremony this week, Dr. Ellen Cohan shared with our students and parents several characteristics of successful people. As she did so, I was reminded of our instructional staff. According to Hal Urban (1992), successful people do the following:

- Accept life as it is, with all its difficulties and challenges. They adapt to it, rather than complain about it. They accept responsibility for their own lives instead of blaming or making excuses.

- Develop and maintain a positive attitude toward life. They look for good in others and in the world, and usually seem to find it.

- Build good relationships. They are sensitive to the needs and feelings of others. They have a way of bringing out the best in other people.

- Have a sense of direction and purpose. They set goals, accomplish them, and then set new goals. They accept and enjoy challenges.

- Have a strong desire to learn. They see learning as a joy, not a duty. They continually enrich their lives by learning new things and improving themselves.

- Are action oriented. They get things done because they are not afraid of hard work, and they don't waste time.

- Maintain high standards in their personal conduct. They know that honesty is one of the main ingredients in the character of a good person.

- Understand the difference between existing and living and always choose the latter. They get the most out of life because they put the most into it; they enjoy life to the fullest.

While I listened to Dr. Cohan sharing these insights into success, I thought of so many of you. I asked her if I could borrow the book so that I could pass this on in our final 2004–2005 Friday Focus. Thank you for consistently exuding success in your personal and professional lives. Thank you, also, for passing these traits of success on to our students throughout this school year. It is an honor to be affiliated with professionals of your stature. As we wrap up another successful year at OMS, I am reminded that it is our people, not our programs, that make a difference. You have made a difference in many lives this year; thanks for making a difference in my own. This summer, I hope you all *Play with Passion!*

Have an awesome weekend!

Jeff

Overtime!

I have loosely organized the contents of this book around the analogy of the school year to an athletic contest divided into four quarters. If the 180 student school days make up the four quarters of regulation time, our summer "break" certainly becomes the overtime period for administrators and other school leaders who work throughout the year planning for and implementing school improvement plans. For the school principal working year-round, the summer months provide a wonderful opportunity to reflect on what has occurred throughout the year. First, it is important to note our many successes, documenting in writing the specific ways in which our schools changed for the better. It is useful to survey all staff just prior to the year's end and review these staff perceptions at the beginning of the summer. Although principals will, of course, want to ask teachers which areas within the school still need improving, it is equally important to simply ask the question, "How has our school improved over this past year?" Too often, we discuss only what we need to work on next and in which areas we are falling short of our goals. We must also celebrate how far we have advanced.

In reviewing teacher survey responses and evaluating our school's performance from an administrative perspective, along with scrutinizing all available school data profiles, certain themes that will merit the attention of school leaders become evident. During the next several weeks, the principal should begin formulating an initial plan for school improvement for the following school year. Elmore (2003) insists that nearly all schools are staffed by teachers and administrators who are working hard. However, not all schools are working on the right work. The "overtime" period is when principals should analyze all quantitative and qualitative school data in an effort to determine exactly what the "right work" is for their particular school in the subsequent year. In the 2004–2005 school year at our own school, I was serving as a first-year principal and had two assistant administrators who were also new to their roles. This, then, was a year for focusing on cultivating a school culture of collegiality and collaboration. We wanted to set the stage for long-term school improvement by working to create a new vision supported by shared values, while still improving our school during the current year in several critical areas. In many ways, we felt that we accomplished our immediate goals and set the stage for the realization of our long-term goals.

As principal, I was already looking forward to the next school year and the next 37 Friday Focus writings that would accompany it. Our business of teaching and learning is very much a cyclical profession. We experience the excitement of Opening Day, the anticipation of the holiday season, the winter doldrums, the spring testing dates, and the satisfaction of completing another successful school year. The weekly Friday Focus writings at our school are one more way in which we mark and enhance the cyclical nature of the school year. Just as our teachers anticipate Thanksgiving and Spring Break, they begin to anticipate the weekly Friday Focus appearing in their in boxes each Friday morning. This small addition to our school helped to improve our school a great deal in just its first year of implementation.

For principals interested in establishing a weekly Friday Focus communication similar to the one that I have shared within these pages, there are many variations they might try. For instance, at the time this book was published, we had completed our second year of the current Friday Focus model and were planning a slightly different version for year three. In our third year of Friday Focus writings, we will focus on one theme for the entire year, examining one component of this large, schoolwide theme throughout the year. There are many teaching and learning books that come to mind which would lend themselves to a yearlong study, examined through weekly Friday Focus writings composed by the school principal and other school leaders.

Regardless of how one utilizes the Friday Focus tool, it is certain to cultivate what Marzano, Waters, and McNulty (2005) call a purposeful community: "one with the collective efficacy and capability to develop and use assets to accomplish goals that matter to all community members through agreed-upon processes" (p. 99). At our school, as we entered into our second year of incorporating the Friday Focus writings as one small, but consistent, way of improving our school, we feel that we have accomplished many goals related to matters that are important to nearly all members of our school community. Most importantly, we feel that we have nurtured a feeling of collective efficacy—or what Marzano, Waters, and McNulty call simply the shared belief that together we make a difference. Through this year of Fridays, our school had indeed made a difference in the lives of our students and each other.

References

Adams, H., & Johnson, S. A. (1997). The teacher's little instruction book: Little bits of wisdom from teachers for teachers. Tulsa, OK: Trade Life.

Albert, L., & DeSisto, P. (1995). *Cooperative discipline.* Circle Pines, MN: American Guidance Service.

Allen, R. H. (2002). Impact teaching: Ideas and strategies for teachers to maximize student learning. Boston: Allyn & Bacon.

Barth, R. (1990). Improving schools from within: Teachers, parents, and principals can make the difference. San Francisco: Jossey-Bass.

Bissell, B. (1992). *The paradoxical leader.* Paper presented at the Missouri Leadership Academy, Columbia, MO.

Blanchard, K., Lacinak, T., Tompkins, C., Ballard, J., & Blanchard, K. (2002). *Whale done!: The power of positive relationships.* New York: Free Press.

Borowski, E. J., & Borwein, J. M. (2002). *Collins dictionary: Mathematics.* Glasgow, UK: Collins Harper.

Brainard, E. (2001). Classroom management: Seventy-three suggestions for secondary school teachers. *Clearing House, 74*(4), 207.

Bransford, J. D., Brown, A. L., & Cocking, R. R. (Eds.). (2000). *How people learn: Brain, mind, experience, and school.* Washington, DC: National Academy.

Carlson, R. (1997). Don't sweat the small stuff—and it's all small stuff. New York: Hyperion.

Clark, R. (2003). The essential 55: Rules for discovering the successful student in every child. New York: Hyperion.

Collier, V. P. (1995). *Acquiring a second language for school.* Washington, DC: National Clearinghouse for Bilingual Education.

Collins, J. (2001). Good to great: Why some companies make the leap...and others don't. New York: HarperCollins.

Covey, S. R., Merrill, A. R., & Merrill, R. R. (1996). *First things first: To live, to love, to learn, to leave a legacy.* New York: Free Press.

Cummins, J. (1984). Bilingualism and special education: Issues in assessment and pedagogy. Clevendon, UK: Multilingual Matters.

Davenport, P., & Anderson, G. A. (2002). *Closing the achievement gap: No excuses.* Houston, TX: American Productivity & Quality Center.

DuFour, R., DuFour, R., Eaker, R., & Karhanek, G. (2004). *Whatever it takes: How professional learning communities respond when kids don't learn.* Bloomington, IN: National Education Service.

DuFour, R., & Eaker, R. (1998). *Professional learning communities at work: Best practices for enhancing student achievement.* Alexandria, VA: Association for Supervision and Curriculum Development.

Eaker, R., DuFour, R., & DuFour, R. (2002). *Getting started: Reculturing schools to become professional learning communities.* Bloomington, IN: National Education Service.

Elmore, R. (2003). Knowing the right thing to do: School improvement and performance-based accountability. Washington, DC: NGA Center for Best Practices.

Fraser, B. J., Walberg, H. J., Welch, W. W., & Hattie, J.A. (1987). Syntheses of educational productivity research. *International Journal of Educational Research, 11,* 145–252.

Georgia Department of Education. (2005). *Georgia ESOL resource guide.* Retrieved January 10, 2005, from http://www.glc.k12.ga.us/panp/esol/resguide.htm

Granrose, J. (2001). Life's meaning. In F. Stephenson (Ed.), *Extraordinary teachers: The essence of excellent teaching* (pp. 43–58). Kansas City, MO: Andrews McMeel.

Harris, R. (1991, March 2). Some ideas for motivating students. *Virtual Salt.* Retrieved January 12, 2005, from http://www.virtualsalt.com/motivate.htm

Hirsch, S. (2002). Leadership begins with thoughtful consideration. *Results,* National Staff Development Council, February 2002.

Hord, S. M. (1997). *Professional learning communities: Communities of continuous inquiry and improvement.* Austin, TX: Southwest Educational Development Laboratory.

Horsch, P., Chen, J., & Wagner, S. L. (2002). The responsive classroom approach: A caring, respectful school environment as a context for development. *Education & Urban Society, 34*(3), 365–384.

Hughes, C. A., Schumaker, J. B., Deshler, D. D., & Mercer, C. D. (1993). *The test-taking strategy.* Lawrence, KS: Edge Enterprises.

Illinois Education Association. (2000). *Tips for more successful parent conferences.* Springfield, IL: IEA-NEA.

Johnson, D. W., & Johnson, R. T. (1989). *Cooperation and competition: Theory and research.* Edina, MN: Interaction Book Company.

Kentucky Migrant Technology Project. (1997). *The classroom teacher's ESL survival packet*. Retrieved January 10, 2005, from http://www.migrant.org/esl/survival_packet/index.cfm

Linn, R. L., & Grunland, N. E. (2000). *Measurement and assessment in teaching*. Columbus, OH: Merrill.

Lundin, S. C., Paul, H., & Christensen, J. (2000). *FISH! A remarkable way to boost morale and improve results*. New York: Hyperion.

Manna, P. (1999, Nov. 17). Hooked on a feeling. *Education WeekAQ, 19*(12), 47.

Marzano, R. J., Pickering, D., & Pollock, J. E. (2001). *Classroom instruction that works: Research-based strategies for increasing student achievement*. Alexandria, VA: Association for Supervision and Curriculum Development.

Marzano, R. J., Waters, T., & McNulty, B. A. (2005). *School leadership that works: From research to results*. Alexandria, VA: Association for Supervision and Curriculum Development.

Maxwell, J. C. (1998). The 21 irrefutable laws of leadership: Follow them and people will follow you. Nashville, TN: Thomas Nelson.

McEwan, E. K. (2003). *7 steps to effective instructional leadership*. Thousand Oaks, CA: Corwin.

National Middle School Association. (1995). *This we believe: Developmentally responsive middle-level schools*. Columbus, OH: Author.

National Staff Development Council. (2001). *NSDC standards for staff development*. Oxford, OH: Author.

Olweus, D. (1993). *Bullying at school: What we know and what we can do*. Cambridge, MA: Blackwell Publishers.

Partin, R. (2004). Classroom teacher's survival guide: Practical strategies, management techniques, and reproducibles for new and experienced teachers. San Francisco: Jossey-Bass.

Project CRISS. (2005). Project CRISS general info: An overview of Project CRISS. Retrieved December 15, 2005, from http://www.projectcriss.com/prc/pages/general_info/overview.html

Rice, G., & Taylor, G. (2000). The peanut butter and jelly guide to teaching. Vicksburg, MS: ETSI.

Sagor, R. D. (1992). Three principals who make a difference. *Educational Leadership, 49*(5), 13–18.

Saphier, J. (2005). Effort-based ability. In R. DuFour, R. Eaker, & R. DuFour (Eds.), *On common ground* (pp. 85–113). Bloomington, IN: National Education Service.

Schlechty, P. (2002). Working on the work: An action plan for teachers, principals, and superintendents. San Francisco: Jossey-Bass.

Spitalli, S. J. (2004). The don'ts of student discipline. *Education Digest, 70*(5), 28–31.

Stenmark, J. K. (1991). *Mathematics assessment: Myths, models, good questions, and practical suggestions.* Reston, VA: National Council of Teachers of Mathematics.

Stephenson, F. (Ed.). (2001). *Extraordinary teachers: The essence of excellent teaching.* Kansas City, MO: Andrews McMeel.

Tomlinson, C. A. (1999). *The differentiated classroom: Responding to the needs of all learners.* Alexandria, VA: Association for Supervision and Curriculum Development.

Traina, R. (1999). What makes a good teacher? *Education Week, 18*(9), 34.

Urban, H. (1992). Life's greatest lessons: Twenty things I want my kids to know. Redwood City, CA: Great Lessons.

U.S. Department of Education. (2004). Early warning, timely response: A guide to safe schools. Retrieved October 1, 2004, from http://www.ed.gov/about/offices/list/osers/osep/gtss.html

Wang, M., Haertel, G., & Walberg, H. (Dec. 1993/Jan. 1994). What helps students learn? *Educational Leadership, 51*(4), 74–79.

Whitaker, T. (2002). What great principals do differently: Fifteen things that matter most. Larchmont, NY: Eye on Education.

Whitaker, T. (2004). What great teachers do differently: Fourteen things that matter most. Larchmont, NY: Eye on Education.

Whitaker, T., & Lumpa, D. (2004). *Great quotes for great educators.* Larchmont, NY: Eye on Education.

Whitaker, T., Whitaker, B., & Lumpa, D. (2000). Motivating and inspiring teachers: The educational leader's guide for building staff morale. Larchmont, NY: Eye on Education.

Wong, H., & Wong, R. (1998). *The first days of school: How to be an effective teacher.* Mountain View, CA: Harry K. Wong.